A GUIDE TO THE EUCHARIST

THE PASCHAL SACRAMENT

Francis Selman

A Guide to the Eucharist

The Paschal Sacrament

Family Publications

Oxford

Abbreviations

CCC   *Catechism of the Catholic Church* (1992).

DS   Denzinger-Schönmetzer, *Enchiridion Symbolorum*, 34th Ed.

LG   *Lumen Gentium.*

ND   Neuner-Dupuis, *The Christian Faith.*

PL   Migne, *Patrologia Latina.*

SC   *Sacrosanctum Concilium.*

ST   Aquinas, *Summa Theologiae.*

To Robert Ombres

ISBN 1-871217-57-1

Cover Picture: Communion of the Apostles, Fra Angelico,
Florence, Museo di San Marco
© 1990. Photo SCALA, Florence.

Frontispiece: Courtesy of Fr Jeremy Fairhead

published by
Family Publications
6a King Street, Oxford, OX2 6DF
www.familypublications.co.uk

printed in England

Contents

Foreword

Father Francis Selman, whom the Dominican Order is proud to count as one of its priest-tertiaries, has written a vigorous study of Eucharistic doctrine. It is based on Scripture, the Fathers, and St Thomas, with occasional references to modern divines and more than occasional citations of recent popes. He covers all the principal themes this sacrament suggests – Real Presence, Eucharistic sacrifice, the bond between the Eucharist and the Church, and the correspondence between the earthly and the heavenly Liturgy. Although the tone is serene he does not scruple to enter the lists with writers whose positions he sees as in some way truncating, or at any rate obscuring, that account of the Holy Sacrifice which best fits the tradition. Recent ecumenical 'agreed statements' come in for this rough treatment too, though, as the author shows, what is problematic about such statements is usually what they do not say rather than what they do. The mistake, if such there be, lies, then, with those who wrongly take these statements to be an exhaustive evaluation of the present-day thinking of the Catholic Church. That, they are not, and cannot claim to be.

It is essential for us to be orthodox, to think with the Church. But then the question arises, What are we to do with sound reflection on this mystery? This is where I find Father Selman's final chapter especially valuable. It is not enough to give assent to doctrine, we must turn it through spiritual labour into a spur to virtue and a ladder for ascent to God. Those who have observed the author's regimen of life will not be surprised to find that here is where his heart is.

Aidan Nichols OP

11

Preface

This book is based on the course book I wrote on the Eucharist for Maryvale Institute, Birmingham. Some parts have been rewritten, and the whole has been expanded with new material. Since the Second Vatican Council was about the Church, writing about the Eucharist after the Council has especially been about how the Eucharist makes the Church and is the sign of the unity of the Church. The Eucharist is called '*the* mystery of faith', but what especially requires faith is not so much that it is the sacrament of the unity of the Church as that the Body and Blood of Christ are really present in the Eucharist. I hope that this book may renew attention to the Real Presence, which is perhaps the most difficult aspect of the Eucharist to explain. My hope is that what I have written may also lead to devotion. Thus the book concludes with a chapter on the grace of the Eucharist in our daily lives. In it I trace the Eucharist from its origins in the Passover to the final fulfilment of its effects in us at our resurrection. The Eucharist is indeed the paschal sacrament.

I am very grateful to Dr Petroc Willey at Maryvale for making available the disk of the course book for my use. My thanks go to Mrs Ann Weston and Mrs Anne Walsh, for typing the course book. I am especially grateful to Josie Callaghan for all the work in producing the expanded version of the original typescript for this book; without her generous help I could not have brought the present book to the publishers. I also thank Mary Aldridge for help with corrections. Fr Aidan Nichols OP has kindly and generously provided the Foreword to the book. Lastly, I thank Colin Mason of Family Publications for accepting this book, his continual encouragement and wise editing, and for saving me from some errors.

January 2006   Francis Selman

Introduction

As we consider the various aspects of the Eucharist one by one in the chapters ahead, it is good to keep in mind its place in the overall life of the Church and its relation to the other sacraments. The Eucharist stands 'at the centre of the Church's life.'[1] The Second Vatican Council called it 'the fount and culmination of the whole Christian life,' and said that it is 'the summit towards which the activity of the Church is directed ... the fountain from which all her powers flow.'[2] All her preaching is directed towards leading people to the Eucharist; at the same time the Eucharist is the centre of the lives of those entrusted with her mission. In its document on the priesthood, the Second Vatican Council said: 'In the Eucharist the entire spiritual good of the Church is contained, namely Christ himself, our Passover and living Bread ... The Eucharist stands forth as the source and culmination of the whole work of evangelisation.'[3] Similarly, Pope John Paul II wrote that the Church draws the power for her mission from perpetuating the sacrifice of the cross and from communion with the Body and Blood of Christ.[4]

For St Thomas Aquinas (1225-1274), 'The source of the whole Christian life is Christ. So this sacrament perfects the others by joining us to Christ.'[5] All the other sacraments are directed towards receiving or consecrating the Eucharist. By Baptism we are incorporated into Christ's body, the Church, so that we may receive his Body. Baptism is the first step because it also removes original sin, which is an obstacle to grace. Likewise, the sacrament

---

1. CCC 1343.
2. LG 2,11.
3. *Presbyterorum Ordinis* 5.
4. *Ecclesia de Eucharistia* 2, 22.
5. *In Sent. IV* d.8 q.1 art.1.

of Penance removes sin and restores grace when it has been lost by sin. The sacrament of Confirmation enables the faithful to play their full part in the life of the Church. Confirmation equips us to witness to the Faith before others. The union of husband and wife in marriage reflects the union of Christ with his bride, the Church, that is symbolised by the Eucharist. The Anointing of the Sick, like Penance, removes sin, and either restores the sick person to full life in the Church or gives food (viaticum) for strength on the last stage of the journey in this life. Ordination is for consecrating the Eucharist. It is the Eucharist which gives us full union with Christ. Thus it is 'the perfection, as it were, of the spiritual life and the term of all the sacraments.'[6] It has been called 'the sacraments of sacraments'.[7]

The Eucharist is the greatest of the sacraments because, unlike the other six sacraments, which only apply the *power* of Christ, this one also contains Christ himself. The other sacraments only occur by being applied to someone: there is no baptism without water being poured on someone, or confirmation without someone being anointed with oil. But the sacrament of the Eucharist already exists with the consecration, for the Body and Blood of Christ are truly present even before they are received in communion. Only in this sacrament, do we adore Christ himself.

The Eucharist is founded on the mystery of the Incarnation, by which the Son of God united human nature to himself. As the Son of God took to himself our humanity so that we might share in his divinity, so his human nature is a source of life for us through its union with divine nature in him. As St Thomas observes, grace is derived for us from the divinity of Christ through his humanity.[8] Christ has left us the sacrament of his humanity, because he is the Way for us to the Father as he is man: 'No one comes to the Father,

---

6. ST 3a 73,3.
7. CCC 1211.
8. Ibid., 3a 62,5.

except through me' (Jn 14:6). We come to the Father through his humanity. His humanity is the one door through which we enter into the pasture of eternal life (Jn 10:7). When Christ withdrew his body from our sight at his Ascension into heaven, he left us his body really present in the sacrament of the Eucharist in an invisible way that we only apprehend by faith. 'Blessed are those who do not see, yet believe' (Jn 20:29).

When we celebrate the Eucharist we re-enact what Christ did at the Last Supper, and what Christ did at the Last Supper was to leave us the means of recalling the Passion he was about to undergo for our salvation on the following day. What Christ did at the Last Supper was to enact his Passion in advance. 'On the night that he was betrayed', he handed himself over to us just as he was about to be handed over into the hands of men. This was notably summed up for us at the Second Vatican Council when it said that at the Last Supper 'Our Saviour instituted the Eucharistic sacrifice of his Body and Blood. He did this in order to perpetuate the sacrifice of the cross throughout the centuries until he should come again.'[9] The Eucharist, however, does not just recall the death of Our Lord but the *whole* Paschal mystery: his death, Resurrection and Ascension, as Pope John Paul emphasises several times in his encyclical on the Eucharist. 'The Eucharist is in an outstanding way the sacrament of the Paschal mystery.'[10] In the same paragraph, he says that the sacrament of the Paschal mystery stands at the centre of the Church's life. Similarly, Pope Benedict XVI has written that the Last Supper, the Cross and the Resurrection form the one indivisible Paschal Mystery.[11]

Benedict XVI sees the Last Supper as an anticipation of Christ's death. At the same time, Christ transformed the meaning of his death into an act of love by the words he spoke over the bread and

---

9. SC 47.
10. *Ecclesia de Eucharistia* 3, 12, 14.
11. *Journey towards Easter* (New York, Crossroad, 1987) p. 108.

the cup, "given up for you" and "poured out for many", which indicate that his death was a voluntary self-sacrifice.[12] 'In the Eucharist we receive this love.'[13] For Benedict XVI, our communion in the Eucharist is founded on a prior communion between God and man in Jesus Christ through the Incarnation. This prior communion becomes communicable to us in the Paschal Mystery. It is the Eucharist which enables us to participate in the Paschal Mystery: 'the inmost mystery of communion between God and man is accessible in the sacrament of the Body of the Risen One.'[14] 'The Eucharist effects our participation in the Paschal Mystery.'[15] Indeed Christ can communicate the Paschal Mystery to us because of his Resurrection: 'To have risen from the dead means to be communicable; it signifies being the one who is open, who gives himself.'[16] Thus the Eucharist is the sacrament of the Paschal Mystery for Benedict XVI, as Christ through his Resurrection became open in a new way to communicating the love which he showed in his voluntary sacrifice and death. Christ initiated this sacrament of the Paschal Mystery at the Last Supper.

We shall begin, then, by looking at the background of the Last Supper in the feast of the Passover in the Old Testament, and the basis of the Church's doctrine of the Eucharist in the New Testament. We shall next trace the early development of this doctrine in the Fathers of the Church. This will bring us, in chapter three, to the first major controversy about the Eucharist, which led to the rounded doctrine of the Real Presence. In chapter four, we shall consider the Eucharist as a sacrifice. In the following chapter, we ask how the real Body of Christ is related to his mystical body, the

---

12. Ibid., p. 104; cf. J Ratzinger, *God is Near Us* (San Francisco, Ignatius Press 2001) p. 81.
13. Ibid., p. 108.
14. J Ratzinger, *Pilgrim Fellowship of Faith* (San Francisco, Ignatius Press 2005) p. 83.
15. Ibid., p. 82.
16. *God is Near Us*, p. 81.

Church. In the three closing chapters we briefly consider the fulfilment of the Eucharist in the heavenly banquet, the Eucharist in ecumenical dialogue and, at more length, the benefits and grace of the Eucharist, how it affects us in our daily lives.

Chapter 1

The Eucharist in Scripture

From Passover to Eucharist

When Christ instituted the Eucharist at the Last Supper he was not doing something entirely novel, but he took an already existing feast and converted it into something new. For the origins of the Eucharist, we go back to the Old Testament and especially to the feast of the Passover, which is described in Exodus 12:1-27. We are told there that on the 14th day of the first month, which was also the first day of unleavened bread, the Hebrews were to kill a male lamb, of one year and without blemish, in the evening, put some of its blood on the lintel and posts of the door, and eat it with unleavened bread. For on this night the Lord passed through the land of Egypt and slew the first-born of the Egyptians, but he *passed over* the houses which had the blood of the lambs smeared on their doors. The Hebrews were to keep this day as a day of memorial in all future generations (Ex 12:14), and when the children of the family asked what is the meaning of this rite, they were to be told, 'It is the sacrifice of the Lord's Passover' (Ex 12:27).

After the Hebrews had, on that same night, crossed through the Red Sea and entered the wilderness of Sin, they soon began to experience a lack of bread. So the Lord told Moses that he would send them bread from heaven (Ex 16:4). This was the manna, which fell in the morning on six days of the week. On the sixth day they were to collect a double ration for the Sabbath also. The Jews were reminded of the bread that God gave their ancestors in the desert when Jesus fed the Five Thousand and Four Thousand with the loaves he had miraculously multiplied (Mt 14:13-21, 15:32-39; Mk 6:32-44, 8:14-21). The evangelists report that they all ate as much as they wanted and twelve, or seven, baskets of scraps were still left over; this echoes Exodus 16:21, that everyone gathered as much of the manna as he wanted.

St John gives the Feeding of the Five Thousand a clear Paschal meaning by explicitly associating it with the Passover, when he remarks that it occurred at the time of the Passover feast (Jn 6:4). In the explanation he gives of this miracle, the Discourse on the Bread of Life, which fills chapter 6 of his Gospel, John links the multiplication of the loaves with the manna before it and the Eucharist that was to follow it, because he tells us by a series of connected phrases that the true bread from heaven was not the bread which the Jews ate in the desert but the body of Jesus. 'It was not Moses who gave you the bread from heaven; my Father gives you the true bread from heaven. For the bread of God is that which comes down from heaven and gives life to the world' (Jn 6:32-33). Jesus then declares that he is the bread of life (6:35). He later says that the bread of life is his flesh: 'I am the living bread which came down from heaven ... and the bread which I shall give for the life of the world is my flesh' (6:51). The Son of God came down from heaven at the Incarnation by taking our lowly human nature and coming into the world. St John also connects the manna, or bread from heaven, with the sacrifice of the Passover, for Jesus speaks of 'the bread which I shall give for the life of the world'. He gave this bread, which is his flesh, for the life of the world by being sacrificed on the cross and dying in order to save the world.

Thus Jesus' miracles of the feeding of the Five and Four Thousand by multiplying the loaves both look back to the Passover and Exodus in the past, and forward to what he was to do at the Last Supper, when he took bread and gave it to his disciples, saying that it was his body, and likewise shared the cup, saying that it was the cup of his blood shed for them. This is clear from the use of almost the same words for describing Jesus' actions when he fed the crowds and again at table with his disciples at the Last

Supper. For we are told that Jesus 'blessed the bread, broke it and gave it to his disciples' (compare Mt 14:19 with Mt 26:26, and Mk 6:41 with Mk 14:22). These words then passed almost unchanged into the Christian liturgy, as we can see in St Paul: Jesus 'took bread, and when he had given thanks (*eucharistesas*)', he broke it (1 Cor 11:24). But where Matthew and Mark say that Jesus blessed the bread (*eulogesas*) at the Feeding of the Five Thousand, John has 'gave thanks' (*eucharistesas*), thus making explicit the connection of this miracle with the Eucharist.

The New Testament seems to intend us to understand that Jesus changed the Passover feast of the Old Testament into the new rite of the Eucharist, which replaces the Passover for Christians, so that it clearly is the paschal sacrament. St Paul, for example, alludes to the Eucharist when he writes, 'Christ our Pasch has been sacrificed' (1 Cor 5:7). It is not certain, however, and is disputed by scholars, whether the Last Supper was itself a Passover meal. The three Synoptic evangelists agree that it was: 'and they prepared the Passover' (Mt 26:19; Mk 14:16; Lk 22:13). But John puts the Last Supper on the day before the Passover, because he wants Jesus to die at the same hour as the Passover lambs are being slain in the Temple, since Jesus is the Lamb of God for St John (1:29). Likewise, John alone points out that there was no need to break the bones of Jesus on the cross since he was already dead (Jn 19:36), just as the Hebrews were instructed not to break a bone of the Passover lamb (Ex 12:46).

Scholars differ about how to deal with this discrepancy between John and the Synoptic Gospels. Aidan Nichols thinks that the two versions can be reconciled if the Synoptics were following the old date of the Passover but John puts the Last Supper on the new date of the Passover, for there was a split among the Jews in the day of celebrating it. Thus Jesus dies on the Passover (old date) in John, but on the following day according to the Synoptics.[17]

---

17. ST 3a 46, 9 ad 1.

It is interesting to note that Aquinas was aware of the difficulty and discusses the question in detail in the section on Redemption in the *Summa*. His solution is that what John calls 'the day before the Passover feast' Matthew calls 'the first day of the Azymes (unleavened bread)', since a Jewish feast began on the preceding evening.[18] Joachim Jeremias, however, does not think that any of the theories support St John against the Synoptics.[19] For Jeremias, the Last Supper was a Passover meal.

Other scholars play down or dissociate the connection between the Eucharist and the Passover. Raymond Moloney SJ finds the origin of the Eucharist in the Jewish prayers of blessing (*berakah*) rather than in the Passover. He thinks that too much emphasis has been put on the Passover as the basis of the Eucharist, and that blessing is the primary form of prayer in the Old Testament, which then leads to praise, thanksgiving and petition. We have an example of a prayer of blessing leading to thanksgiving for God's mighty deeds in saving his people when Jethro prays, 'Blessed be the Lord, who has delivered us out of the hands of the Egyptians and out of the hand of Pharaoh' (Ex 18:10). Jethro then offers a burnt offering (holocaust) and sacrifices to God. Moloney points out that Jesus *blesses* the loaves before giving them to the Five Thousand, and that the cup passed round at the end of the Passover meal is the cup of blessing. At the Last Supper too, Jesus blesses the bread and breaks it (Mt 26:26; Mk 14:22). It seems rather inconsistent, however, to play down the connection of the Passover with the Eucharist, since *the* great event of redemption in the history of the Israelites for which they thanked and praised God was the Exodus, commemorated at the Passover.

The sound Catholic scholar of Scripture, Xavier Léon-Dufour SJ did not think that the Last Supper was a Passover meal. John Kodell agrees with him, that the Last Supper was not a Passover meal.[20]

---

18. *The Holy Eucharist*, p. 23.
19. *The Eucharistic Words of Jesus*, p. 82.
20. *The Eucharist in the New Testament*, p. 66.

He thinks that, because Jesus knew that he would be overtaken by events on the day of the Passover, he celebrated a Jewish festive meal the night before the Passover. A festive meal, however, hardly seems to fit the mood of the Last Supper when Jesus announced his imminent betrayal and enacted the rite by which his companions were thereafter to recall his passion and death.

The Words of Institution

The New Testament contains four accounts of Jesus' institution of the Eucharist at the Last Supper: Mt 26:26-29; Mk 14:22-25; Lk 22:15-20; and 1 Cor 11:23-26. These four texts may be divided into two groups of two: Matthew resembles Mark, and Luke has similarities with St Paul. There is some dispute about which is the earliest text, but it is generally agreed that Matthew depends on Mark and that Luke either depends on St Paul or independently used the same source as St Paul, which is thought to have existed in Antioch around AD 40 (for St Paul in Antioch, see Acts 11:22-26.) This leaves either Mark or St Paul as the earliest account of the Eucharist. St Paul wrote his first letter to the Corinthians in AD 56, five years after founding the Church there. He clearly brought to them an already existing account of the Last Supper. The agreement of Luke and Paul with Matthew and Mark suggests that the meaning given to Jesus' actions at the Last Supper goes back to Jesus himself. Jeremias has done much to show that these four texts of the institution of the Eucharist were not invented to reflect early liturgical practice but go back to Jesus himself. Although St Paul's may be the earliest *written* account, from AD 56, but using a source from about AD 40, St Mark may well give us the original account that takes us back to the Last Supper itself.

We may note some variations of this view. The Catholic scholar Heinz Schürmann thinks that Luke's account is the oldest, deriving from the same source as St Paul. Rudolf Pesch regards Mark as original and holds that Matthew depended on Mark and Luke copied Mark. This is only the view of a minority today.

At this point, it will be convenient to lay out these texts, in order to have them clearly in sight and to notice their similarities and variations.

Paul, 1 Cor 11:23-26	*Luke 22:19-20*
This is my body which is for you.	This is my body which is given for you.
Do this in remembrance of me.	Do this in remembrance of me.
This cup is the new covenant in my blood.	This cup which is poured out for you is the new covenant in my blood.
Do this, as often as you drink it, in remembrance of me.	

Mark 14:22-24	*Matthew 26:26-28*
Take, this is my body.	Take, eat; this is my body.
This is my blood of the covenant,	Drink of it, all of you; for this is my blood of the covenant
which is poured out for many.	which is poured out for many, for the forgiveness of sins.

We notice straightaway that Mark's is the shortest and most primitive account. The main difference between the two groups is that Paul and Luke have the command, 'Do this in remembrance of me.' Matthew and Mark say that Jesus' blood is 'poured out for many,' which connects Jesus with the Suffering Servant, who poured out his soul to death (Is 53:12). Luke has this phrase in common with the other two Synoptics, but St Paul does not mention it. Matthew adds to Mark that the blood of Jesus is poured out 'for the forgiveness of sins;' Matthew, after all, was the only one of these four present at the Last Supper. Matthew alone, apart from 'Take' in Mark, has the command, 'Take, eat' and 'Drink of it'. Some scholars think that we do not have an account of the Last Supper in 1 Corinthians 11:23-26 but rather a description of an early liturgy. We should note, however, that St Paul prefaces his account by saying that he received from the Lord what he handed on to the Corinthians (11:23). We may recall that St Paul did not receive the Gospel from any man but through a revelation by Jesus Christ (Gal 1:12). All three Synoptics, but not St Paul, have Jesus' saying that he will not drink the fruit of the vine again until he drinks it anew in the kingdom, except that St Luke alone puts the saying before the blessing of the bread and cup (Mt 26:29; Mk 14:25; Lk 22:15-16).

With the words of Jesus at the Last Supper firmly in our mind, we may now pass on from the historical origin of these texts to the meaning of the words that Jesus spoke over the bread and the cup.

The New Covenant

From the beginning the Passover was a sacrifice, since the blood of the lamb that was killed and eaten was put on the doors of the houses of the Hebrews: 'It is the sacrifice of the Lord's Passover' (Ex 12:27). Likewise, when God made the covenant with his people at the foot of Mount Sinai it was sealed with a sacrifice (Ex 24:5). As Moses sprinkled the people with blood from the sacrificed animals at the end of making the covenant, saying 'Behold the blood of the covenant which the Lord has made with you' (Ex 24:8), so Jesus seals the New Covenant, not with the blood of animals, but with his own blood. Thus the making of the Old and the New Covenant went with a sacrifice. To sacrifice literally means 'to make holy'; it is to make something over to God. This is what Christ did with himself at the Last Supper as he was about to give himself up and enter into his passion, which led to his death on the cross. Hebrews 9:20 quotes Exodus 24:8 in a passage which points out that Moses ratified the first covenant with blood just as Christ established the New Covenant with the sacrifice of himself. Thus when Christ said at the Last Supper, 'This is the cup of the new covenant in my blood' (1 Cor 11:25 and Lk 22:20) or 'This is my blood of the covenant' (Mt 26:28 and Mk 14:24), he looked back to the first covenant following the Passover and Exodus, and

showed that he was inaugurating the New Covenant as he celebrated the Passover. In speaking of the *New* Covenant he fulfilled
the promise of New Covenant made by Jeremiah 31:31-34, which
is quoted by Hebrews 8:8-12.

Since the letter to the Hebrews supplies us with much of our
understanding of Jesus' words about the cup as the blood of the
New Covenant, it will be useful here to follow the argument of
chapters 7-10 in this letter. If it had been possible to attain perfection under the Levitical priesthood, there would have been no
need for a new priesthood (7:11). The new priesthood is not of the
order of Aaron but of Melchisedek, and where there is a change
of priesthood there is also a change of law (7:13). Christ is a priest
forever according to the order of Melchisedek (7:17, which appeals
to Psalm 109:4: 'Thou art a priest forever, according to the order of
Melchisedek'). There were many priests, because they died, but
now there is one, because he lives forever (7:23). Since he was sin-
less, his sacrifice is once-for-all and saves for all time. The old law
never made anyone perfect, because its priests had repeatedly to
offer sacrifices but Christ's is once for all as he is holy and blame-
less (7:26-27). Since the first covenant was not without fault (8:7),
it has been replaced by a new covenant, which was promised by
the Old Law itself. The New Covenant makes the old one obso-
lete (8:8-13). The sanctuary of the Temple was but a copy of the
sanctuary not made with hands (8:5). As the high priests of the
Old Covenant entered the Holy of Holies once a year, so Christ
has entered the heavenly sanctuary once for all, taking with him
his own blood (9:12, 24). Even under the first covenant, blood was
used to purify everything; so Christ's blood is much more effective to purify our consciences than the blood of bulls and goats
(9:11-14). Christ's sacrifice is a better one, since he does not need
to offer sacrifices repeatedly like the priests of the Old Covenant,
for he suffered once (9:26). As he died once, there is only one sacrifice (9:28). God did not anyway take pleasure in the sacrifices of
animals but he is pleased with the obedience of the one who came

to do his will by offering his own body (10:5-10). (Obedience is a sacrifice of one's own will.) Thus Christ sanctifies the people for all time by a single sacrifice for sins (10:12). The New Covenant, promised in Jeremiah 31:33, is also an everlasting one, which will not be superseded like the first one, because Christ offered the perfect sacrifice of himself and, having entered the heavenly sanctuary, lives forever. Just as the high priests used to pass through the veil of the curtain of the Temple, so we now enter the heavenly sanctuary through the veil of his flesh, with the blood of Jesus (Heb 10:20).

Hebrews makes two special points about the value of blood in sacrifice. First, blood purifies, so it is *expiatory*: that is, it atones for sins: 'without the shedding of blood there is no forgiveness of sins (Heb 9:22). Secondly, Christ's sacrifice is also propitiatory: he intercedes for us for all time with his Father by the single sacrifice of himself (Heb 7:25, 9:25). These two points were to be taken up by the Council of Trent. We should also note that, for the Hebrews, the life was in the blood (Lv 17:11; Dt 12:23). So to drink Christ's blood by sharing his cup is also to receive a share in his life.

The blood with which Christ seals the New Covenant expiates sin. We can see that Christ attached this meaning to the shedding of his blood from the words for the cup recorded by Mark 14:24 and Matthew 26:28: 'which is poured out for many.' This phrase recalls the Song of the Suffering Servant: 'yet he bore the sin of many' (Is 53:13). This verse of Isaiah also lies behind a pivotal saying in St Mark: the Son of man came not to be served but to serve 'and to give his life as a ransom for many'(10:45). The words that Jesus spoke over the cup at the Last Supper show that he is that Servant who suffers in the place of sinners 'for many.' As the Israelites were redeemed from slavery in Egypt by the blood of the Paschal lamb, which they sacrificed and put on the door posts of their houses, so we are redeemed by the blood of Christ, who gave his life 'as a ransom for many.' We may note some further similarities between the words of Jesus about shedding his blood 'for many' and 'for the forgiveness of sins' (Mt 26:28) and the Song of the Suffering Servant. The Servant 'makes himself an offering for sin' (Is 53:10) and he 'pours out his soul' to death (Is 53:12). The Suffering Servant is virtually identified with the innocent Lamb of God, and so with the Passover Lamb, because he is 'like a lamb that is led to the slaughter and like a sheep that is dumb before its shearers (Is 53:7). The Paschal lamb and the Suffering Servant come together in Christ. St Peter may well have had this identification of the Paschal lamb with the Suffering Servant in mind when he wrote, 'you were ransomed with the precious blood of Christ, like that of a lamb' (1 Pet 1:18-19).

As the Jews remembered the saving deeds by which God redeemed his people out of Egypt at the feast of the Passover, so Christians recall the events of their redemption by Christ at the Eucharist, when they do what Christ did at the Last Supper. The Hebrews were told that the feast of the Passover was to be a *memorial* day, a day of remembering their redemption from Egypt (Ex 12:14). The eating of unleavened bread at the Passover, as the people did on the night they crossed out of Egypt, was also to be a 'memorial' (Ex 13:9). They were to *remember* that once they were slaves in Egypt (Dt 16:12). Likewise, the Eucharist is to be celebrated in memory of Christ's redeeming sacrifice, as the command of Jesus to do this 'in my memory' (*eis ten emen anamnesin*) indicates (Lk 22:19; 1 Cor 11:24, where the words are attached to 'This is my body').

This remembrance, or *anamnesis*, however, is not merely the recalling of an event in the past but is also entering into and reliving the past event. As Colman O'Neill puts it, *anamnesis* 're-actualises' the saving event.[21] Thus it is an effective memorial, which makes God's saving deeds present. In giving thanks (*eucharistein*) for what God has done for us in redeeming us by the death and resurrection of his Son, Jesus Christ, these saving events are made

---

21. *New Approaches to the Eucharist*, p. 57.

present for us. All this is contained in the word *eucharistesas* (having given thanks), which Matthew and Mark use for the blessing of the cup, and Luke and Paul use for the blessing of the bread, adding 'and likewise taking the cup'. Thus, *anamnesis*, in the biblical sense, is not merely to repeat something past but, in some way, to make a past event present across time. Christians will carry on doing this until the end of time, because 'as often as you eat this bread and drink this cup, you announce the death of the Lord until *whenever he comes*' (1 Cor 11:26).

Thus the Eucharist not only recalls the past, making it present again, but also looks forward to the future, when Christ will come again. A reference to the future is contained in all three narratives of the Eucharist in the Synoptic evangelists. Matthew and Mark conclude the words of institution thus: 'I tell you that I shall not drink henceforth of the fruit of the vine until that day when I shall drink it new with you in the kingdom of my Father'. Thus the Eucharist anticipates the Messianic banquet in heaven, as promised in Isaiah 25:6-9. But Luke 22:15 puts the words looking forward to the future fulfilment of the Eucharist in heaven *before* the words of institution: 'I tell you that I shall not eat it (the Pasch) until it has been fulfilled in the kingdom of God'.

Jesus alludes to the heavenly banquet in Matthew 8:11 and, in a different context, in Luke 13:29: 'Many will come from East and West and sit at table with Abraham, Isaac and Jacob in the kingdom of heaven'. The parable of the Wedding Feast given by the King for his Son also directs us to the heavenly banquet (Mt 22:1-14; Lk 14:16-24). The wedding feast given for the son then becomes the Marriage Feast of the Lamb in heaven in Revelation 19:9. This book ends with the call of the Spirit and the Bride, 'Come' (Rev 22:17), which reflects the same prayer in the Eucharist of the early Church for Christ to come, as we find it expressed in its Aramaic form in St Paul: '*Maranatha*' (1 Cor 16:22).

Although I have mainly discussed the meaning of Christ's words over the cup, particularly as 'the blood of the new covenant,' which is 'poured out for many', the significance of the words over the bread has already partly been treated in the previous section on the miracle of the Feeding of the Five Thousand, with its background in the Exodus. We return to the same theme with the Discourse on the Bread of Life in St John, chapter six.

The Bread of Life

It is remarkable that, although the Last Supper takes up over one sixth of St John's Gospel, from chapters 13-17, there is almost no direct reference to the Eucharist in it, with the possible exception of the parable of the true Vine (15:1-11). There may be several reasons for this. First, the whole of St John's Gospel may be regarded as *paschal*. The Last Supper itself begins with Jesus saying that it is now time for him to cross over from this world to his Father (13:1). His return to the Father through his Passion is his Passover. Perhaps John also thought that the words of institution, given by the three Synoptics, were already well known and established, but what was needed was Jesus' own explanation of the Eucharist, which is lacking from the Synoptics. For this we turn to the Discourse on the Bread of Life in chapter six of St John. The important verses are 6:51-58. This chapter both looks back to the Passover, for it contains Jesus' explanation of the Feeding of the Five Thousand, which St John specially notes took place at the time of the Passover, and forward to the Last Supper, for he talks about the bread that he shall give for the life of the world (6:51). Thus St John combines the two themes of the Passover and of sacrifice in chapter six. We may discern in the words 'for the life of the world' an allusion to the institution of the Eucharist, which are St John's equivalent for 'given up for you' and 'poured out for many', for clearly giving up his life for the life of the world means giving himself in sacrifice.

In chapter six, St John presents the Eucharist primarily as food and drink. But this food and drink are clearly Jesus' own flesh and blood: 'unless you eat the flesh of the Son of man and drink his blood ... whoever eats my flesh and drinks my blood' (6:53-54).

31

There is a clear identity of what is eaten and drunk in the Eucharist with the flesh and blood of Christ. Aidan Nichols speaks of this same 'identity' of the Eucharist with the body and blood of Christ in the words of institution in the Synoptic Gospels.[22] He remarks that bread and wine are not just symbolic of Christ's body and blood. St John makes clear that the Eucharist is not merely symbolic when Jesus says: 'My flesh is true food and my blood is true drink' (6:55). The word used for 'true' here is *alethinos* which means 'real'. Thus these words support the Catholic belief in the Real Presence: what we receive in the Eucharist is the true Body and Blood of Christ. John Paul II has commented on these same words, that the Eucharist is not metaphorical but real food and drink.[23] Aidan Nichols draws attention to the remarkable expression of Jesus, 'whoever eats *me*' (6:57). This makes plain that we do not share in bread and wine in the Eucharist but receive Christ himself.

St John also tells us more than the other evangelists about the benefits of the Eucharist for those who receive it. These benefits are principally three. First, whoever eats his flesh and drinks his blood dwells in him (6:56). This indwelling is mutual: we are in Christ and Christ is in us. The pattern of our dwelling in Christ is his own dwelling in the Father: we are in him as he is in the Father (Jn 17:21). Secondly, as Christ draws his life as man from the Father through the union of his human nature to divine nature in his person, so we draw life from Christ through his human nature by eating his flesh and drinking his blood: 'As I live through the Father, so whoever eats me will live through me' (6:57). As Christ draws life from the Father, so we share in his divine life through sharing in his flesh and blood. Thirdly, the Eucharist gives us a share in eternal life even now. For eternal life, in the Gospel of St John, is not just future, but a certain kind of life, the real life which

---

22. Op. cit., p. 27.
23. *Ecclesia de Eucharistia* 1, 16.

Christ gives to those who believe in him. The sharing in eternal life already in this life provides us with a pledge of our resurrection on the Last Day (6:54). This connection of the Eucharist with the resurrection of the body was drawn out by some of the Fathers of the Church, as we shall see in the next chapter.

In laying the foundation of the doctrine of the Eucharist in the ground of Scripture, it remains for us to note two further aspects of the Eucharist in the Acts of the Apostles. We are told there that the first Christians 'persevered in the teaching (*didache*) of the Apostles and in the common life (*koinonia*), the breaking of bread and prayers' (Acts 2:42). Thus the Eucharist was commonly called 'the breaking of bread' to begin with. In Acts 2:46, we are told that they 'broke bread' in their homes and, in Acts 20:7, that they were gathered together 'to break bread' on the first day of the week, that is, on the day that the Lord rose again. The same phrase, 'the first day of the week', is used by St Mark at the beginning of his account of the Resurrection (Mk 16:2). The word *koinonia* means communion and has recently become an important word in ecumenical dialogue as it readily provides a way of understanding the Church as a communion of people. It is also used by St Paul when he says that the cup we bless is a participation (*koinonia*) in the blood of Christ and the bread we break a participation in the body of Christ (1 Cor 10:16-17). From this participation in Christ St Paul draws the moral lesson that Christians are not also to have communion (*koinonia*) with demons or idols (1 Cor 10:20).

In this chapter, I have shown that the Eucharist goes back to the Passover. The Passover combines the two elements of sacrifice and bread from heaven. These two prefigure the double aspect of the Eucharist as a sacrifice and communion. Moreover, Christ seals the New Covenant with his blood 'poured out for many' in sacrifice. The miracles of feeding the people with the loaves both looked back to the bread from heaven in the desert and forward to the Last Supper. The Eucharist too has a past, present and future dimension. It is the memorial or *anamnesis*, of Christ's redeeming sacrifice and death on the cross, as it now replaces the feast of the Passover which was the memorial of the event by which God first redeemed his people at the Exodus from Egypt. It gives us food and drink in the present life as it is a communion with the body and blood of Christ. At the same time, the Eucharist also looks forward to its future fulfilment in the heavenly banquet and to the time when Christ will come again. As St Thomas Aquinas has neatly summarised this past, present and future significance of the Eucharist: it is a memorial of Christ's passion in the past, it gives us grace in the present, and leads us to the future life of glory in heaven.[24]

---

24. ST 3a 73, 4.

Chapter 2

The Eucharist in the Fathers

In the Patristic Age, say from AD 100 to St Gregory the Great (d. 604), we find little consistent and sustained attempt by the Church to work out her doctrine of the Eucharist. This was because her energies during this time were primarily taken up by defending the true nature of the Trinity and the person of Christ. It was not until the 11th century that debate about the Eucharist came to the forefront of the Church's attention. Thus the Fathers of the Church provide the first tentative steps towards constructing a doctrine of the Eucharist, but often with little reference to one another and only in short texts. In all this time, no whole work devoted to the Eucharist was produced, except the relevant parts of the catechetical instructions of Gregory of Nyssa, Cyril of Jerusalem and Ambrose. The Eucharist in this period, then, is a prime example of doctrine being discussed in the course of the Church's ordinary day-to-day preaching rather than in the more academic and philosophic controversies about Christ and the Trinity. Nevertheless, where we can trace a thread through the Fathers on the Eucharist, certain clear outlines emerge, which contain all the fundamental elements of the Church's later doctrine. We observe the development of a doctrine. The disparity of the sources for the Eucharist in the Fathers itself witnesses to the homogeneity of faith about the Eucharist that existed in widespread parts of the Mediterranean world in late ancient times.

Aidan Nichols divides views about the Eucharist among the Fathers into two basic groups, which he calls the realist and the symbolist. Realists said that the bread *is* the body of Christ, and the wine *is* the blood of Christ. Symbolists said that bread and wine are symbols, figures or types of the body and blood of Christ.

Fr Nichols cautions, us, however, against thinking that symbolists then were what we would call symbolists today, because a symbol for the ancients was not merely a symbol but partook itself in the reality it represented.[25] Thus to say that a writer in the Age of the Fathers was a symbolist is not to say that he thought the Eucharist was a mere figure or that he did not believe in the Real Presence. This explanation of symbol is supported by Fr Moloney, who points out that symbol and reality were not quite distinct for the ancients, since the symbol participates in the reality.[26] Use of the word 'symbol' enabled Christians in the early Church to express the belief that Christ's glorified body in heaven and his body in the Eucharist are the same yet differ. A symbolist was closer to a realist then than now. Sometimes both views are found in the same author. Eventually, however the realist view triumphed over the symbolist view of the Eucharist.

St Ignatius of Antioch

Our first witness after the Apostolic Age for the presence of Christ in the Eucharist is St Ignatius of Antioch (d. 107). He is an unequivocal realist, who identifies bread with the flesh of Christ, and the Eucharist with the crucified and risen body of Christ.

> The Eucharist is the flesh of our Saviour, Jesus Christ, who suffered for our sins.[27]

The body in the Eucharist is identical with the body which hung on the cross. Ignatius stresses the reality of Christ's body against the Docetists, who held that Christ only *seemed* to have human nature.

Here 'Eucharist' is used for the sacrament itself rather than for the liturgical action of giving thanks. The identification of the elements with the flesh and blood of our Saviour is itself based

---

25. Op. cit., p. 35.
26. Op. cit., p. 99.
27. *Smyrnans* 7,1.

on the central verses of John 6:52-58. Ignatius mentions people who 'abstain from the Eucharist and prayer, because they do not believe that the Eucharist is the flesh of our Saviour Jesus Christ'. Another important text in Ignatius, linking the Eucharist with the unity of the Church, is his letter to the Ephesians 20:

> Be careful to observe one Eucharist, for there is only one flesh of Our Lord Jesus Christ, and one cup of union with his blood, one altar of sacrifice.

Here union with Christ is connected with union with the Church.

St Justin

Properly speaking, Ignatius belonged to the sub-apostolic age, and Justin to the Apologists (second half of the 2nd century) rather than to the Fathers. Like Ignatius, Justin came from the Eastern region of the Church and was martyred in Rome c. 165. Thus Justin witnesses to the liturgy in Rome in the middle of the 2nd century. Justin sees that it is possible for bread and wine to become the body and blood of Christ just as the Word descended into the womb of Mary and became flesh, and as bread and wine are changed into our flesh and blood when we consume them. Justin makes the same identification of the Eucharist with the body and blood of Christ as Ignatius of Antioch does.

> For we do not receive these as common bread and common drink; but as Jesus Christ our Saviour, having been made flesh by the Word of God, had both flesh and blood for our salvation, so likewise we have learned that the food over which thanks has been given by prayer of the word comes from him, and by which our blood and flesh are nourished through a change (*metabolen*), is the flesh and blood of the same incarnate Jesus.[28]

---

28. *Apology* I c. 66.

Although Justin, for the first time, speaks of a change here, we should note that he does not explicitly speak of the change of bread and wine in the Eucharist but of the change of food when we digest it and it becomes part of our body by metabolism. Even in the natural process of metabolism we see how elements can lose their own being in becoming part of our bodies. A similar analogy was taken up by Gregory of Nyssa in the fourth century.

St Irenaeus

St Irenaeus may be regarded as the first great theologian of the Church after the writers of the New Testament. Like Ignatius of Antioch and Justin, he too came from the Eastern end of the Mediterranean and ended in the West, as Bishop of Lyons, where he was martyred c. 200. But where Justin links the Eucharist with the Incarnation, Irenaeus links it with the Resurrection, just as Jesus himself speaks of rising again in connection with the living Bread (Jn 6:39, 40, 44, 54).

> As bread and wine receive the Word of God and become the body and blood of Christ, so our flesh will rise incorruptible through being nourished by his body and blood.[29]

For Irenaeus, it is the Word of God, that is, Christ or his words, which makes bread and wine be the body and blood of Christ.

> As the vine ... and as the grain of wheat ... having *received* the Word of God become the Eucharist, which is the body and blood of Christ; so also our bodies, having been nourished by the Eucharist, shall rise at their time, the Word of God granting them resurrection.[30]

> So our bodies, receiving the Eucharist, are no longer corruptible but have the hope of resurrection to eternal life.[31]

---

29. *Adversus Haereses* V 2,2.
30. Ibid., V 2,3.
31. Ibid., IV 18,5.

Irenaeus is the first to mention the change of bread and wine in the Eucharist; he says that they 'become' (*gignetai*) the body and blood of Christ.

> Just as the bread of the earth, on receiving the invocation (*epiklesin*) of God, is no longer ordinary bread but the Eucharist.[32]

Irenaeus is also the first to mention the role of the epiclesis at the consecration of bread and wine. These are variously changed by the Word and by the invocation of the Holy Spirit in Irenaeus.

One of Irenaeus' main aims in writing about the Eucharist was to defend the goodness of material creation against the Gnostics, who were dualists and regarded all matter as intrinsically evil, for they did not recognise it as the creation of the good God but thought it came from some principle of evil. It is impossible to include sacraments in your religion if you do not think that the material creation used in them is good or comes from God. Matter cannot be a medium of grace unless it is good in itself. Irenaeus' response to the Gnostics was that the material creation must be good, because we use material elements in the sacraments, so that bread, wine, water and oil become means of receiving divine life.

In spite of these lapidary references to the Eucharist in the second century, one or two definite themes begin to stand out. For all three writers, the Eucharist clearly *is* the body and blood of Christ: it is not ordinary bread or wine (this point will be repeated by Cyril of Jerusalem). Ignatius of Antioch and Irenaeus draw their thought about the Eucharist from Chapter 6 of St John: their thought is Johannine. We now pass on to the time after the Council of Nicaea in AD 325, and deal first with three Eastern Fathers before two Western Fathers (SS Ambrose and Augustine). We shall conclude with St John Damascene, who sums up the Eastern tradition until the seventh century.

---

32. Ibid., IV 18,5.

St Gregory of Nyssa (c. 335-394)

The main source for St Gregory of Nyssa's teaching on the Eucharist is his Thirty-seventh Catechetical Oration. His most important contribution to thought about the Eucharist is the various words he proposed for describing the change of bread and wine: *metapoiésthai* (to be transformed) and *metastoicheiousthai* (to be transelemented). This second term means that there is a change of the elements of the sacrament (bread and wine) rather than a change of substance, which became the way that the Church spoke later.

> Rightly then do we believe that the bread consecrated by the Word of God has been changed (*metapoiésthai*) into the body of the Word of God.[33]

> As Christ assumed bread and wine into his body on earth, so now he assumes bread and wine into his body and blood at the consecration by the power of the blessing.[34]

We have already noticed a similar comparison in St Justin: since bread and wine were changed into Christ's natural body when he lived on earth, they can now be changed into his body and blood in the sacrament. This happens, St Gregory says, when the Word comes to dwell in the bread. The bread is transformed into Christ's body by means of the word of the Word, "This is my body".

We also find in Gregory of Nyssa the idea that God can change the nature of things.

> He gives these things (a share in incorruption) through the power of the blessing, by which he transelements (*metastoicheiosas*) the nature of things that are apparent.[35]

Gregory of Nyssa, like Irenaeus in the second century, associates the Eucharist with our resurrection. Our body cannot become

---

33. *Cat. Orat.* 37,9.
34. Ibid.
35. Ibid., 37,12.

immortal unless it shares in incorruptibility through communion with the immortal body of Christ.

St Cyril of Jerusalem (314-386)

St Cyril's *Mystagogic Catecheses* 4 and 5, on the Eucharist, are the Twenty-second and Twenty-third of his Catecheses. They are evidence for the liturgy in Jerusalem towards the end of the fourth century. Cyril variously says that the bread *becomes* the body of Christ and wine the blood of Christ, and that bread *is* the body of Christ and wine *is* the blood of Christ.[36] He also states that the Eucharist is a communion in the body of Christ and a partaking of the blood of Christ.[37]

> Therefore, with all confidence we receive this as the body and blood of Christ. For in the type (*tupo*) of bread the body is given to you, and in the type (*tupo*) of wine the blood is given to you, so that partaking of the body and blood of Christ, you may become one body and blood with Christ.[38]

Here we meet symbolism side by side with realism. The Greek word *tupos* (type), when used for the Eucharist, is equivalent to the Latin *figura*, a figure. Here St Cyril is using 'type' in the way that we say 'under the appearances of bread and wine'. We notice in this passage too, that by receiving Christ's body we are made one body with him: that is, by receiving his real body we become his mystical body, the Church. Union with Christ in the Eucharist produces the communion of the Church. But more about this theme in chapter five.

St Cyril continues the same passage with what are perhaps his best known words about the Eucharist, quoted by Paul VI in *Mysterium Fidei* 48:

---

36. *Myst. Cat.* 4.
37. *Myst. Cat.* 5.
38. Ibid., 4,3.

> You have been taught and fully instructed that what seems to be bread is not bread, even though it appears to be such to the sense of taste, but the body of Christ; and what appears to be wine is not wine, even if taste thinks it such, but the blood of Christ.[39]

Here we have Cyril of Jerusalem contrasting the *appearances* of bread and wine with the reality of Christ's body and blood in the Eucharist. St Cyril likens the change in the Eucharist to the change of water into wine: 'Once by his own will, he changed water into wine at Cana of Galilee; is he not worthy of belief when he changes (*metabolon*) wine into blood?'[40]

St John Chrysostom

To complete our sample of the Eastern (Greek) Fathers in the fourth and early fifth centuries, we now compare the Antiochenes, represented by St John Chrysostom and Theodore of Mopsuestia, with the Alexandrians, represented by St Cyril of Alexandria. The main differences between the two schools was, that the Antiochenes emphasised the humanity of Christ and the Alexandrians his divinity. In Theodore of Mopsuestia (d. 428), bread and wine remain in the Eucharist, but in the Alexandrians they are changed. Theodore gives two apparently conflicting accounts. On the one hand, he says:

> He did not say "This is a symbol of my body" and "This is a symbol of my blood" but rather "This is my body and blood", thereby teaching us not to look at the nature of what is here before us, but through the event of the Eucharist it is changed into his flesh and blood.[41]

Theodore here implies that a change of the nature, or being, of bread and wine occurs in the Eucharist. He also rejects a merely

39. Ibid., 4,9.
40. Ibid., 4,2.
41. *Homily* 15,10.

symbolic understanding. On the other hand, in the same homily, he writes:

> For when you are eating, you are not eating bread and wine but the *antitype* of the body and blood of Christ.

An antitype is more like a figure. St John Chrysostom (c. 349-407), however, clearly states that bread and wine are changed. He uses the word *metaskeuazein*, which means to alter, refashion. The priest speaks the words, but the power and grace belong to God, ' "This is my body", he says; this sentence transforms the offerings.'[42]

A change in Chrysostom's own approach to the Eucharist took place at about the time he was transferred from the see of Antioch to Constantinople. Up to 400, he emphasised that the Eucharist is a participation in the heavenly liturgy. After 400, he considers it primarily as the sacrifice of the cross. How these two aspects can be united will be mentioned in chapter six.

St Cyril of Alexandria (370-444) also says that the elements of the sacrament are transformed. The chief point to note in his teaching about the Eucharist is that it is the life-giving flesh of Christ. In this he was clearly influenced by St John (6:51-58).

> What has truly been offered is transformed in a hidden way by the all-powerful God into Christ's body and blood. And when we have become partakers of Christ's body and blood, we receive the life-giving, sanctifying power of Christ.[43]

Elsewhere he writes:

> The flesh is life-giving because it is assumed by the Word.[44]

Cyril argued against Nestorius that the Eucharist could not be life-giving unless the Word assumed human nature into the unity

---

42. *Hom. in Matt.* 82,5.
43. *In Matt.* 26,27.
44. *Comm. in Ioann.* 6,64.

of his person and did not, as Nestorius held, just dwell in the man Jesus as God dwells in a temple.

St Ambrose (c. 335-397)

St Ambrose, who knew Greek and was influenced by Origen, employs the scheme of Plato, in which things in this world are images of realities in a higher world. Thus the Old Testament contains *shadows* of the New Testament (cf. Heb 10:1). And things in the New Testament are *images* of the *truth* in heaven. The New Testament already contains the reality, but it is hidden (*in mysterio*); the truth (*veritas*) is not yet plain to our sight. For this scheme St Ambrose could also appeal to 1 Cor 10:4-6: all ate the same supernatural food and drank the same supernatural drink from the rock, which was Christ. These things were types (*tupoi*) for us, St Paul says. As the Hebrews ate manna in the desert, so we now eat the true bread from heaven in the Eucharist. We have figures or types in the Old Testament, sacraments of heavenly grace in the New.

One of St Ambrose's most important passages on the Eucharist will be kept for the next chapter, as it is quoted by Aquinas. It is about the power of God's creative Word to change the things he has created in the first place. He vividly speaks of the power of God's word thus:

> If the word of Elijah had such power as to call down fire from heaven, will not the word of Christ have power to change the nature of the elements?[45]

> The sacrament you receive is brought about (*efficitur*) by the word of Christ.[46]

> The sacraments, through the mystery of the sacred prayer, are transfigured into his flesh and blood. [47]

---

45. *De Mysteriis* 52.
46. Ibid., 52.
47. *De Fide* IV 10,24.

The Eucharist is the true body of Christ and this body is identical with the body which hung on the cross.

> The true flesh of Christ is the body that came from the Virgin, was crucified and buried; therefore truly this is the sacrament of that flesh.[48]

In summary, then, Ambrose explicitly teaches that a change occurs in the Eucharist and that the body present in the Eucharist is identical with the body born of the Virgin, suffered on the cross and was raised up again from the tomb. It is the flesh of this body that is our food in the Eucharist.

St Augustine (354-430)

St Augustine frequently touches on the Eucharist, but usually in connection with the Church. Thus I shall reserve most quotations from him on the Eucharist for chapter five, on the Mystical Body of Christ. Augustine does not discuss the Real Presence in the Eucharist, because he increasingly considers *the whole Christ*, Head and members together. This is Christ's body, the Church. Augustine's preoccupation with the unity of the Church was the result of his greatest pastoral concern, which was the Donatist schism in Northern Africa.

St Augustine's lack of attention to the Real Presence may in part be explained by two reasons. First, he could take it for granted in his congregation at Hippo. Secondly, Raymond Moloney suggests that, because Augustine was a Platonist in his philosophy, there is a certain dualism in his thought about the Eucharist. Christ's real body is in heaven, because it can only be in one place; so his body on earth is the Church, the whole Christ. Thus he says:

> He who suffered for us has entrusted to us in the sacrament his body and blood, which indeed he has even made us. For we have been made his body and, by his

---

48. *De Mysteriis 53.*

mercy, we are that which we receive.[49]

In other words, we become what we receive in the Eucharist, his body. The Eucharist makes us into what we receive: the body of Christ.

We may also note a striking insight of Augustine. He says that when we drink from the chalice we drink 'the price of our redemption', because the price Christ paid to buy us back from slavery to sin was his own blood. The idea may well be inspired by 1 Peter 1:18-19: 'we have been ransomed with the precious blood of the Lamb'. 'You know the price that was paid for you' Augustine says in *Sermon 9*, 10. At the banquet of the Eucharist, Christ feeds his guests with himself for food; the one who invites is also the food and drink of the banquet.[50]

Augustine's other major contribution to the doctrine of the Eucharist, that it is the sacrifice offered by the Church, will be laid out at the beginning of chapter four.

St John Damascene (d. 649)

We may suitably conclude this brief survey of the key stages in the development of the doctrine of the Real Presence among the Fathers with St John Damascene, who summed up the teaching of the Greek Fathers in his *De Fide Orthodoxa*. John of Damascus, who lived in a monastery near Jerusalem, also wrote a work in defence of images against the Iconoclasts. As the Iconoclasts held that no images should be made of Christ and that the only acceptable image of him is the Eucharist, the orthodox were compelled to reject any suggestion that the Eucharist is a figure or symbol, and to assert the realist view. Thus the deacon Epiphanius spoke out at the Second Council at Nicaea in 787, saying that the Eucharist is not an image (*eikon*) but the very body and blood of Christ.[51]

---

49. *Sermon 229*.
50. *Sermon 329*, 1.
51. A Nichols, *The Holy Eucharist*, p. 41.

John Damascene too made it clear that the Eucharist is more than an icon of Christ; it is the reality itself. 'The bread and wine are not a type of the body and blood of Christ (may no one say that); rather it is the very deified body of the Lord. He himself said, "This is my body", not "This is a type of my body".'[52]

John of Damascus takes up the earlier idea of Justin, that as the Word was made flesh by entering the womb of the Virgin, so bread is made into the body of Christ when the Word comes upon it.

> As the Word of God was able to create and make flesh for himself from the Virgin, why should he not be able to make bread his body and wine and water his blood? He does this through his all-powerful command.[53]

Damascene attributes the change in the Eucharist to the epiclesis rather than to the consecration. The words of consecration are in the indicative (This is my body), but the invocation of the Holy Spirit is like a command (Let your Spirit come upon these gifts).

> Through the invocation (*epikleseos*) it, namely the over-shadowing power of the Holy Spirit, becomes like rain to a newly planted land. For just as all that God made he made through the power of the Holy Spirit, so now these things which surpass nature ... are made by the power of the Spirit. "How shall this happen to me?" said the holy Virgin ... The Archangel Gabriel replied, "The Holy Spirit will come upon you, and the power of the Most High will overshadow you." And now you ask how the bread becomes the body of Christ and the wine and water his blood. I say to you: the Holy Spirit is present and does these things.[54]

Here John Damascene ascribes the change of bread and wine to the power of the Holy Spirit at the epiclesis, just as the Word was

---

52. *De Fide Orth.* IV 13.
53. Ibid., IV 13.
54. Ibid., IV 13.

made flesh when the Holy Spirit came upon Mary and overshad-
owed her. Elsewhere, he attributes the change to the creative
word of God working with the Holy Spirit.

> And we know nothing more except that the Word of
> God is true and effective and all-powerful ... However,
> it is not inaccurate to say that, just as in nature bread
> and wine and water are changed (*metaballontai*) into the
> body and blood of the one who eats and drinks, ... so the
> bread that has been set forth and the wine and water,
> through the invocation and coming of the Holy Spirit,
> are supernaturally transformed (*metapoiountai*) into the
> body and blood of Christ and are not two things but one
> and the same.[55]

Thus Damascene excludes the opinion that bread and wine remain, and identifies the Eucharist with the body and blood of
Christ.

In the liturgy of the Eastern Orthodox Church the epiclesis
is highlighted; this is the high moment in the Eucharist rather
than the consecration, as in the Roman Church, which puts the
emphasis on the *words* of Christ as effecting the change of bread
and wine. Is it possible to combine these two different approaches:
the power of the Holy Spirit or the words of consecration? Little
connection has been apparent in the Western theology of the
Eucharist, but by turning to the Old Testament on creation we
can see how the two approaches may be made compatible. The
co-operation of the Word with the Holy Spirit is already seen at
the creation of the world, when the Spirit hovered over the waters
which God created by his Word.[56] In the Old Testament, the Spirit
is associated with the Word in the work of creation: 'You spoke
and they were made. You sent forth your Spirit and it formed
them' (Jud 16:14). 'By his word the heavens were made, by the

---

55. Ibid., IV 13
56. Gen 1:2.

breath (spirit) of his mouth all the stars' (Ps 32:6). In a similar way, the Holy Spirit and the Word work together in changing bread and wine in the Eucharist.

To return to John Damascene, he was the first to say that we receive the divinity of Christ with his body and blood, because they are 'hypostatically' united, that is, in one person, through the Incarnation. As the two natures, divine and human, are inseparably united in the person of Christ, so we share in his divine nature by receiving his body and blood.

> For his body and blood are joined to the godhead hypostatically, and the two natures are joined inseparably in the unity of person in the one body of Christ that we receive. Therefore, we are made sharers of both natures.[57]

This was later to be expanded into the phrase 'body, blood, soul and divinity'. By receiving the first two, we receive all four, for what is not separated in Christ is not separated in the Eucharist.

> The body that is from the holy Virgin is truly united to the divinity, not that the body taken up into heaven comes down, but rather this bread and wine are changed (*metapoiountai*) into the body and blood of God.

John Damascene, then, clearly speaks of the *change* of bread and wine into Christ's body and blood at the Eucharist. He combines the roles of the Holy Spirit and the creative Word in effecting this change. What is hypostatically united in the person of Christ is also received in communion. John Damascene takes up ideas from the tradition before him, which are later used by St Thomas Aquinas. From the East we now turn to the West in the early Middle Ages, to the first major controversy about the Eucharist and the consequent development of the doctrine of the Real Presence.

---

57. *Third Discourse on Images*, PG 94, 1348.

Chapter 3

The Real Presence

Before we trace the steps by which the Church developed her doctrine of the Real Presence in the Eucharist, we do well to recall that Christ's presence is not limited to the Eucharist and that there are *several* modes of his presence. The Second Vatican Council teaches that Christ is present in *four* ways, but pre-eminently in the Eucharist. First, he is present in his priest; secondly, and especially, in the Eucharist, thirdly, in the proclamation of his word; fourthly, in the Church at prayer – 'Wherever two or three are gathered in my name'.[58] We are talking about the presence of Christ's humanity in the Eucharist; there is no need for a sacrament of his divinity, because as God he is anyway present everywhere. But his glorified body is in heaven, 'seated at the right hand of the Father' since his Ascension. Colman O'Neill argues for the bodily, and so real, presence of Christ in the Eucharist, because this is the way that we are most present to one another. The presence of two people in the same room is a bodily one. O'Neill sees a series of degrees, corresponding to the above four ways of Christ's presence, leading up to his bodily presence in the Eucharist. First, Christ *acts* through his priests. Secondly, in the Eucharist we have his *sacramental* presence, that is, beneath the signs of the sacrament. In the preaching of the Word we have the *mission* of Christ, who sent out his disciples just as he was sent by the Father into the world. Fourthly, we have the Church as *a community of faith* when she is gathered in prayer. 'Man meets man through the medium of the whole body', O'Neill writes.[59] But he

---

58. SC 7.
59. *New Approaches*, p. 64.

adds that the corporeal aspect of our contact with Christ in this life is only achieved through symbolic signs. '"Bodily" presence signifies immediate, local presence, and this is not realised in the sacrament.'[60] St Thomas gives a further reason for Christ leaving us his bodily presence in the Eucharist. It belongs to friends to share a common life and so to eat together. As Christ shared in our human nature out of love, 'it corresponded with the love of Christ, out of which he assumed a body of human nature for our salvation', that he should give us his body in the Eucharist.[61]

There are two principal questions connected with the Real Presence in the Eucharist:

1. What is present in the Eucharist? Is it merely bread and wine or some other reality not visible to the sense of sight?

2. And how does it come to be present in the sacrament?

The first question is answered by the doctrine of the Real Presence; the second by 'a wonderful change'.[62]

From Paschasius to Berengar

The first controversy about the Eucharist in the Church arose through the reaction of various people to what Paschasius Radbertus had written in his *De Corpore et Sanguine Domini*, in 831, the first treatise on the Eucharist. Paschasius (c. 790-865) was Abbot of Corbie in North East France. He wrote his treatise in response to two questions put to him by King Charles the Bald:

1. Is Christ present in the sacrament in mystery or in truth?

2. Is the body in the sacrament the same as the body born of the Virgin?

Paschasius' answer to the first question was that the Eucharist is Christ's body and blood in truth. To some, however, Paschasius

---

60. Ibid., p. 65.
61. ST 3a 75,1.
62. Trent XIII, canon 2; ND 1527.

seemed to give a too literal interpretation of Christ's words about eating his flesh, as though they meant that we physically bite Christ's body with our teeth. It should be noted that Paschasius qualifies his unequivocally realist view by adding that it is to be understood in a spiritual, not carnal way. Paschasius distinguishes between the *appearances*, which are those of bread and wine, and the *truth* of the sacrament, which is the body and blood of Christ. For the truth we could also say the reality of the sacrament: what it is in truth it is in reality. Paschasius supports his view with the argument that, as it is the body in the New Testament, it is not merely a figure, for figures belong to the Old Testament, but the truth.[63]

In answer to the second of Charles the Bald's two questions, Paschasius takes up the passage from St Ambrose, *De Mysteriis* 53, already quoted in chapter two. The body in the sacrament is identical with the body that was born of the Virgin, suffered on the cross and rose from the tomb.

> This body and blood of Christ, which is his true flesh and true blood in the mystery, although it remains in the figure of bread and wine, is altogether nothing other than that which was born of Mary, suffered on the cross and rose from the tomb.[64]

This thought is enshrined in the motet, beginning:

> *Ave verum corpus natum de Maria Virgine;*
> *vere passum, immolatum in cruce pro homine.*

(Hail, true body born of the Virgin Mary, that truly suffered, was sacrificed on the cross for mankind.) This motet is variously ascribed to an unknown author c. 1310 and to Pope Innocent IV (1352-1362), so around the middle of the fourteenth century.

Paschasius also explains the change by the same appeal to the overshadowing of Mary at the Annunciation that we found in

---

63. *De Corpore et Sanguine Domini*, c. 4, 1 (PL 120, 1278).
64. Ibid., c. 1, 2 (PL 120, 1269).

John Damascene at the end of the previous chapter:

> But if you truly believe that flesh to have been created from the Virgin Mary in the womb without seed by the power of the Holy Spirit, so that the Word became flesh, truly believe that also what is effected by the word of Christ through the Holy Spirit to be his body from the Virgin.[65]

Here we have a hint of a change of substance in the Eucharist.

The first to object to Paschasius Radbertus' treatise was one of his own monks at Corbie, Ratramnus, who argued that, as the truth is openly set forth for everyone to see, but the body of Christ is hidden in the sacrament and what is hidden is a figure, not the truth, so the Eucharist is a figure of Christ's body and blood. 'Substantially the bread is not Christ, nor the wine Christ. These are a figure.' For Ratramnus, to be 'in the sacrament' is equivalent to being 'in a figure.' Ratramnus proposed that Christ is 'spiritually' present in the Eucharist. There is some ground for this view in St Augustine, *Tract. in Ioannem* 26,11, but it is clear that Augustine talks there about *receiving* Christ spiritually and understanding the doctrine in a spiritual, not carnal or gross, way.[66] Augustine means the way *we* receive Christ, not the way Christ himself exists in the sacrament. By receiving Christ spiritually, Augustine means the person with a good disposition, 'who eats in his heart, does not just press with his teeth'. Augustine adds that teeth break the sacrament but faith *savours* it.[67] Aquinas later explained that, when Augustine said that Christ is spiritually present in the sacrament, he meant that he is present 'invisibly and by the power of the Holy Spirit'.[68] The objections made by Ratramnus were revived 200 years later by Berengar of Tours in the middle of the eleventh century.

---

65. Ibid., 4, 3 (PL 120, 1279).
66. *Tract. in Ioann.* 26, 11.
67. Ibid., 26,12.
68. ST 3a 75,1.

Berengar of Tours (c. 1010-1088) was understandably concerned that, if bread and wine are no longer present in the sacrament, no sign is left, but every sacrament is by its nature a sign. Berengar seems to have held a view close to that of Luther 400 years ahead of the Reformation, that bread and wine become the body and blood of Christ 'for faith and understanding'. This makes Christ's presence in the Eucharist depend on the faith of the individual, not on an objective reality that depends on the power of the word of God. Berengar held that we eat Christ's body in a sign. He was called to abjure his views at the Council of Rome in 1079, when he accepted the formula proposed by Gregory VII:

> I, Berengar, believe with my heart and confess with my mouth that the bread and wine, which are placed on the altar, are substantially converted by the mystery of sacred speech and the words of our Redeemer into the true and proper life-giving body and blood of Jesus Christ our Lord, and after the consecration are the true body and blood of Christ, which was born of the Virgin, offered for the salvation of the world, hung on the cross and is seated at the right hand of the Father; and the true blood of Christ which was poured from his side, not only by the sign and virtue of the sacrament but in their own nature and true substance.[69]

This was the first time that the Church spoke of a substantial conversion or change of the bread and wine in the Eucharist. Gregory VII used 'substance' to oppose Berengar's view that the Eucharist is a figure of Christ's body and blood. It is not clear, however, that Berengar really changed his mind, or what he exactly believed, for he continued not to admit that there was any change of bread and wine themselves.[70] His view thus remained close to Luther's later theory of consubstantiation: Christ is present with bread and wine.

---

69. DS 700; ND 1501.
70. A Nichols, *The Holy Eucharist*, p. 62.

Berengar was opposed by Lanfranc (c. 1010-1089), Archbishop of Canterbury, in his treatise with the same title as that of Paschasius, *De Corpore et Sanguine Domini*, written in 1065. In this treatise, Lanfranc teaches:

> The Church, spread throughout the whole world, confesses that the bread and wine are placed on the altar for consecration, but during the consecration are incomprehensibly and ineffably changed (*commutari*) into the substance of (Christ's) flesh and blood.[71]

Lanfranc contrasts substance with appearances (*species*) and qualities, which are the features of the sacrament that are perceived by the senses.[72] He says that the body in the sacrament is the same as Christ's glorified body in heaven, but they differ in appearance: what exists in the sacrament is 'essentially the same, though there is much discrepancy in their qualities.'[73] Bread and wine do not remain, as the substance of snow does remain when it is changed into ice.

Lanfranc emphasises the power of the words of consecration to change bread and wine. 'The sacrament you receive,' he says, 'is made by the word (*sermone*) of Christ. As the divine blessing has greater power than nature, this sacrament is what the blessing has consecrated, and not the bread that nature formed.'[74] He quotes the passage of St Ambrose, given in the previous chapter and later to be quoted by Aquinas, about God's power to change the whole being of a thing, and at the same time affirms the creative power of God's word to change the nature of things by appealing to Psalm 32:9: 'He spoke and they were made'.

Almost contemporary with Lanfranc was the little known but notable Guitmund of Aversa (d. circa 1090). In his treatise *De Corporis et Sanguinis Veritate in Eucharistia,* he teaches that 'the bread

---

71. *De Corpore et Sanguine Domini* c. 8 (PL 150, 419).
72. Ibid., c. 18 (PL 150, 430c).
73. Ibid., c. 4 (PL 150, 424).
74. Ibid., c. 18 (PL 150, 431).

and wine are substantially changed (*substantialiter commutari*) into the body and blood of the Lord.'[75] The substantial body of Christ is present, and, through communion, Christ is *substantially* in us, not only by concord of will.[76] Eventually, the word *mutare* and its cognates were dropped in favour of *conversio* for naming the change that takes place in the Eucharist.

Lanfranc and Guitmund, then, mark an important stage in the development of Eucharistic doctrine by confirming the tendency to speak of a change of substance. Not just bread and wine are changed, as in the Fathers, but their substance is changed, so that Christ is *substantially* present. This latter phrase was taken up by St Thomas Aquinas and adopted by the Council of Trent. A change of substance makes explicit the change of being that St Ambrose had already spoken of to his catechumens. Substance was also used to counter the view that the Eucharist is just a figure or symbol of Christ's body. Thus a change of substance goes with claiming that the Eucharist is the *true* body and blood of Christ, as is implicit in John 6,55: 'my flesh is real food and my blood real drink.'

It was but a step for the Church to take from saying that bread and wine are 'substantially converted' at the synod of Rome in 1079 to using the word 'transubstantiate' for the first time at the Fourth Lateran Council in 1215: 'when bread has been *transubstantiated* into his body and wine into his blood by divine power.'[77] For a full explanation of transubstantiation we now turn to St Thomas Aquinas, who was born ten years after the Fourth Lateran Council. In his doctrine of the Eucharist, Aquinas brings together ideas and expressions that we already find in Paschasius, Lanfranc and Guitmund and may therefore be said to have become part of the Church's tradition in the West, which Aquinas found ready to hand before him.

---

75. PL 149, 1488 B.
76. Ibid., 149, 1434 B.
77. DS 802 (my italics). This is omitted by Neuner-Dupuis, who, however quote an earlier letter from 1202, in which Innocent III used the word 'transubstantiate' (ND 1502).

Aquinas and Transubstantiation

St Thomas Aquinas (1225-1274) begins his questions on the Eucharist in the *Summa* (3a qq. 73-83) by remarking that just as we have a sacrament of spiritual birth (baptism) and another for spiritual growth (confirmation), so we are provided with a sacrament of spiritual nourishment to maintain our spiritual life. His approach is first to consider the signs, or elements, of the sacrament, which are food and drink, in much the same ways as catechists today begin by teaching children that the Eucharist is a 'meal.' Thus the Eucharist is first of all for St Thomas 'spiritual nourishment' or 'spiritual refreshment'.[78] He notes that the Eucharist is commonly given three names:

1. a *sacrifice*, because it is the commemoration of the Lord's passion;

2. *communion*, because it signifies the unity of the Church;

3. *viaticum*, because it shows us the way to reach the enjoyment of God in our heavenly homeland.[79]

We may note that these three names of the Eucharist correspond with its *past, present and future* aspects. It looks back to the past as we commemorate Christ's passion; it is union with Christ in the present; and it leads us to its heavenly fulfilment in the future.

St Thomas next considers *why* Christ instituted this sacrament, which was at the Last Supper when Christ conversed with the disciples for the last time in his earthly life. So when he was on the point of withdrawing his visible presence from them, he left himself in a sacramental appearance. Secondly, as no one can be saved without faith in the passion of Christ,[80] so he left us a way of representing his passion. The chief sign of this in the Old Testament was the Paschal Lamb: 'Christ our Passover has

---

78. ST 3a 73,1.
79. ST 3a 73,4.
80. Rom 3:25: 'Christ was put forward as an expiation to be received by faith.'

been sacrificed' (1 Cor 5:7). Thirdly, so that we may remember Christ, for the last things that we do with friends before departing are more deeply impressed on their minds.[81] Thus St Thomas straightaway introduces the idea that the Eucharist is a sacrifice as well as spiritual food. It is called a sacrifice, he says, because it represents the Passion of Christ; but it is called an offering (*hostia*), because it *contains* Christ.[82] Thus it is a sacrifice, because Christ is really present in this sacrament.

We next have to ask: in what way, or how, is Christ in the sacrament of the Eucharist? For St Thomas' answer to this question we go to q. 75,1, where his very first words are: 'It must be said that the true body and blood of Christ exist in this sacrament.' Not in a way that can be apprehended by the senses but solely by faith. Aquinas then points out that, as the sacrifices of the Old Testament were only figures of Christ's passion, the sacrifice of the New Law which was instituted by Christ contains something more: Christ himself as having suffered, 'not just in figure but also in the truth of the reality.' Thus this sacrament 'really contains Christ himself.'[83] In saying that Christ *really* exists in this sacrament, Aquinas rejects the view that the Eucharist is just a symbol or figure of Christ's body. The 'inventor' of this view, he says, was Berengar.

The next question, then, is how Christ *comes to be* in this sacrament, which he discusses in the very next article.[84] There are two possibilities, he says, for something to come to be where it was not previously: either by moving to there or by a change of what was there before. Christ, however, does not come to be in the sacrament by moving locally to it, because then it would follow that his body leaves heaven each time. Secondly, as a body can only finish up in one place, not several, when it moves, Christ's body could not be in the sacrament in several places at the same time. So it re-

---

81. ST 3a 73, 5.
82. ST 3a 73, 4 ad 3.
83. ST 3a 75,1.
84. ST 3a 75,2.

mains that Christ's body can only begin to be in the sacrament 'by a conversion of the substance of bread into himself.' St Thomas excludes the opinion that the substance of bread and wine remain after the consecration, because he says that it would take away 'the truth of this sacrament', that the *true* body of Christ exists in it.[85] The view that Christ is present beside bread and wine, which remain after the consecration and so are not changed, is known as *'consubstantiation'*. It is the view most commonly held by Lutherans and some Anglicans.

Expressions which imply consubstantiation may now also be found among Catholics. For example, Paul McPartlan writes of 'the real presence of Christ in the Eucharistic elements of bread and wine.'[86] If Christ is present in the elements of bread and wine, or in bread and wine, then bread and wine remain and they have not been changed. Pope Paul VI gives as the Church's belief that, 'on the conversion of the bread and wine's substance, or nature, into the body and blood of Christ, nothing is left of the bread and wine but the appearance alone.'[87] If consubstantiation were right, however, Christ would not have said "This is my body" but "This bread is my body", as though bread still remained. What is changed into something else does not remain. The substance of bread is not Christ, but what was bread is now the body of Christ. If bread remained, it would be wrong for Catholics to adore the host after consecration, as they do. St Thomas also considers a third possibility, that bread and wine are annihilated and in this way Christ comes to be where he was not before. But he discounts this possibility, because annihilation means that something is turned into nothing, whereas bread and wine are changed into something, namely the body and blood of Christ.[88] In his commentary on the *First Letter to the Corinthians*, Aqui-

---

85. Ibid., 3a 75,2.
86. *The Eucharist* (CTS) p. 26.
87. *Mysterium Fidei* 46.
88. ST 3a 75, 3.

nas presents the various possibilities slightly differently: (1) Christ's body is not present in truth but in a sign or figure; (2) Christ's body is truly present with the substance of bread (consubstantiation); (3) Christ's body comes to be in the sacrament by moving thither (but it would then cease to be in heaven); (4) as none of these three possibilities is admissible, Christ's body truly exists in this sacrament by the change (*conversione*) of bread and wine.[89]

As Christ's body does not move to the sacrament, nor are bread and wine annihilated, Christ begins to be there by 'a change of the substance of bread into himself.' But St Thomas quickly explains that this change is not like a natural one but is 'altogether supernatural, effected solely by the power of God.'[90] In every change, something changes and something remains the same. In a natural change, the same quantity of matter remains as the subject of the change and the outer appearances change. But in the Eucharist it is the other way round: the outward appearances of bread and wine remain the same, but there is a change of the underlying thing. A natural change is a change of form, but Christ, or the form of Christ, does not become the form of what was bread and wine. Rather there is a change of the *total being* of bread and wine in the Eucharist. Thus there is not just a change of form but of substance: that is, a substantial change. St Thomas quotes the words that St Ambrose used in his ordinary instruction to the catechumens in the cathedral of Milan: 'If God can bring things into existence out of nothing, he certainly has the power to change the whole being of a thing into another thing.'[91] In his commentary on 1 Corinthians, Aquinas notes that a natural change is always a change of form, but God is the author of form and matter (because he is the Creator); so he can change the whole substance of a thing.

89. *In 1 Cor* c. 11 lect.5.
90. ST 3a 75,4.
91. *De Sacramentis IV* c. 4,15.

This change is supernatural, because bread and wine have no natural power of their own to turn into the body and blood of Christ. Thus this change is above the power of nature. But God has power over the whole being of things, because he has given them their *whole* being by making them out of nothing in the first place. Thus the change of bread and wine in the Eucharist is founded on God's power of creation. When St Thomas considers the question why the Eucharist is not mentioned in the Creed although it is *the* mystery of faith, he assigns it to the almighty power of God, who has created all things.[92] He says that the change in the Eucharist is both like and unlike creation. It is like creation, because bread and wine have no power to become the body and blood of Christ, just as nothing had the power to become the world before creation. The change of bread and wine is also *instantaneous*, just as creation is instantaneous, and is complete when the last word of each set of consecrating words is spoken over the respective element. Bread and wine are not gradually changed.[93] But the Eucharist is also unlike creation, because it *is* the change of something but creation was not the change of anything already existing, for nothing existed before creation except God.

As God created the world by his Word: 'he spoke and they came into being'(Ps 32:9), so the change in the Eucharist is effected by the words of Christ, who is also God. This is neatly put by St Thomas in his hymn *Pange, lingua, gloriosi* (which ends with the *Tantum ergo*):

> *Verbum caro panem verum*
> *Verbo carnem efficit.*

Literally, the Word made flesh makes bread indeed be his flesh by his word. God's word has *creative* power. The words of consecration are the words of the Word himself, by whom all things were made from nothing. At creation, however, God's word was

---

92. ST 2a 2ae 1, 8 ad 6.
93. ST 3a 75,5.

imperative: "Let there be light", and there was light. Here, in the Eucharist, it is indicative: "This *is* my body", "This *is* the cup of my blood." The words of consecration indicate what has taken place; they both signify the change that has occurred and bring it about. The words are not only *significativa* (signifying) but also *factiva* (active), because they effect what they signify; they bring about what they say has come about.[94] But they do not work just like God's word at creation but *sacramentally*, that is, 'by the power (*vi*) of signification'. So they are not imperative, as at creation, but indicative, for they tell us what has come about beneath the sacramental signs, that is, beneath the appearances of the bread and wine.[95] St Thomas says that the words of consecration effect what they signify. "This", he says, signifies substance, that is to say, what is contained beneath these accidents (appearances) is my body. Only "This" is used, not "This bread is", because there is no common substance between the bread that was there before and what is there now after the change.[96] Similarly, "This" said over the cup stands by metonymy for the contents of the cup: "This is the cup of my blood".[97]

Although the priest utters the words of consecration, we can tell that it is Christ who speaks these words through the priest, because when the priest says "This is my body", he obviously does not mean his own body. The words are, therefore, spoken by the person to whom "my" refers, who is Christ. Pope John Paul II says that Christ speaks the words of consecration as he did in the Upper Room.[98] Through their share in the one priesthood of Christ, validly ordained priests provide the link with the Last Supper.[99] Their priesthood can be traced back through the line of

---

94. ST 3a 78,5.
95. ST 3a 78, 2 ad 2.
96. *In 1 Cor* c. 11 lect. 5 (669).
97. Ibid., c. 11 lect. 6 (677).
98. *Ecclesia de Eucharistia* 5.
99. Ibid., 3, 29.

succession to the Apostles, who received it from Christ at the Last Supper when he said "Do this in memory of me".

St Thomas says that there is a change of the substance of bread into the body of Christ. He uses the word 'substance', because the Church had already adopted it for speaking about the Eucharist; he did not just take it from the philosophy of Aristotle. Before St Thomas, the Church used this word to make clear that the Eucharist was not just a figure of Christ's body but his real body. St Thomas shows us how the word is useful in other ways too. He says that Christ is present in the sacrament 'in the way that substance exists (*per modum substantiae*), to contrast this with being in a place, which is with dimensions that can be measured.[100] Christ is present as substance is present, for the substance of a thing is wholly present in every part and is not affected by its dimensions, whether they be smaller or greater. For example, a fragment broken from a loaf is just as much the substance of bread as the whole loaf is. When Alice drank the bottle of liquid saying "Drink me", she was just as much a human being (or substance) whether she shrank or grew very tall. When we say that Christ is 'substantially' present in the Eucharist, we mean that he is wholly present in every part. 'Substantial', O'Neill says, means 'whole and entire.'[101] Being present 'by way of substance' follows from a change of substance, which goes back to Gregory VII in 1079. Quoting Pope Paul VI, John Paul II also says that 'substantial presence' means that Christ 'is wholly and entirely present.'[102]

The substance of bread is changed in the Eucharist, but the dimensions of the host are not; they remain the same as before. Christ is *contained* beneath the appearances of bread and wine, but his body obviously is not contained in the Eucharist with its own dimensions, with which it was visible on earth and can be seen now in heaven. The word 'substance' enables us to grasp

---

100. ST 3a 76,2
101. *New Approaches*, p. 66.
102. Op. cit., 1, 15.

that Christ's body can be present in the sacrament without its proper dimensions which it has in heaven. Christ does not occupy place, for he does not take up space, but the dimensions of the sacrament do.[103] The dimensions of the sacramental appearances remain the same, just as they appear to our sight, but these are not the dimensions of Christ's body in heaven. I use the word 'appearances' instead of St Thomas' 'accidents', because it is easier to understand and because 'accidents' was replaced by 'appearances' at the Council of Trent. This change is justified by St Thomas' own usage, for he sometimes uses the word '*species*' (appearances) himself .[104]

The *true* body and blood of Christ are present in the sacrament: that is, the same body that suffered on the cross and is now glorified in heaven, 'seated at the right hand of the Father'. It is the same body, but it has a different *mode of existence* in the sacrament. Christ's body is in heaven in its *natural* existence, but in the Eucharist in its *sacramental* mode of existence: that is, beneath the signs of the sacrament, as every sacrament is by its nature a sign. Although it is a sacramental presence in the Eucharist, it is still a *real* presence. Christ's body can be present in the several places at once, in heaven and in the sacrament wherever it is being celebrated, because the sacrament has a *relation* to his body in heaven. This relation ceases when the appearances of the sacrament disappear.[105]

Aquinas also describes Christ's presence in the Eucharist by saying that he is present *beneath* the appearances of the sacrament. For example, he explicitly says that the words of consecration make 'what was contained under these appearances, which was bread, be the body of Christ.'[106]

But Christ is present in an invisible way, hidden from our

---

103. ST 76,5.
104. E.g. ST 75,3 and 5; 77,3 and 7.
105. ST 76,6.
106. ST 78,5.

sight, as he is contained in the sacrament *beneath* the appearances of bread and wine. As St Thomas says in the *Adoro te devote*:

> *In cruce latebat sola Deitas,*
> *At hic latet simul et humanitas.*

That is, on the cross only his deity lay concealed, but here (in the sacrament) his humanity also is concealed at the same time. During his life on earth only Christ's divinity was hidden from men, but in the Eucharist his humanity is hidden as well. The senses do not tell us everything about a thing; they reach no further than the surface and outward appearances. They do not penetrate to the interior of things and know *what* they are. If the senses could reach to everything, there would be no need for faith. But faith passes *beyond* sight in this life. Faith comes in where the senses fall short, as it says in the *Tantum ergo*:

> *Praestet fides supplementum*
> *sensuum defectui.*

May faith provide additional help where the senses fail (for the defect of the senses). The senses do not give us complete knowledge of things. When Christ withdrew his body from our sight at the Ascension, he left a way for it to be present to us, though concealed from sight, in the sacrament. Thus he fulfils his promise to be with us 'always until the end of time' (Mt 28:20) in the Eucharist. Even during the forty days after the Resurrection, Christ had to temper the appearances of his glorified body, in order to be visible to his disciples. So he was not seen the whole time but only when he appeared to them. If Christ were to show us his body in its glorified state, it would be too bright for us to behold. So he now presents his body to us beneath the lowly appearances of bread and wine in the sacrament for the sight of faith.

Many have felt that one of the chief difficulties of St Thomas' explanation of the Eucharist is that the appearances of bread and wine continue to exist without inhering in any substance, for they do not inhere in Christ but the substance of bread and wine no longer exist after the consecration. This doctrine of the appearances, or accidents, existing without their substance is parodied by Lewis Carroll in *Alice in Wonderland*: it is like the smile of the Cheshire cat that continues to be visible in the tree without the body of the cat. St Thomas' way of solving this difficulty is to say that the appearances of bread and wine can continue to exist without their substance, because all things depend anyway more on God to keep them in existence than they depend on secondary causes. The appearances are kept by God with the same existence which they previously had in bread and wine, because God holds everything in existence anyway.[107] Although it is common for people to speak of 'the miracle of the Eucharist', the miracle of the Eucharist for St Thomas was not so much the supernatural change of bread and wine as the continued existence of their appearances without their natural subject.

The signs of this sacrament are not bread and wine, for these no longer exist after the consecration, but the *appearances* of bread and wine.[108] It is the appearances of bread and wine that signify the presence of Christ's body and blood in the Eucharist, not bread and wine, for these have been changed. In his commentary on St John, Aquinas excludes the view that bread and wine are the signs of the sacrament: Our Lord 'insinuates the truth of this sacrament when he says "is my flesh". He does not say "signifies my flesh" but "is my flesh", because what is eaten in reality truly is the body of Christ.'[109] These words of St Thomas also pre-empt, seven hundred years in advance, the theory of transignification, which will be described at the end of this chapter. St Thomas is commenting here on Christ's words "the bread that I shall give is my flesh for the life of the world" (Jn 6:51).

Although the *whole* Christ is present beneath the appearances of either element, so that you receive Christ just as much in the

---

107. ST 3a 77, 1 ad 3.
108. ST 3a 77, 7.
109. *In Ioann.* c. 6 lect. 6.

host alone as with the chalice also, his body is present in different ways beneath the appearances of bread and wine. His body is present beneath the appearances of bread '*by the power of the sacrament*' (*vi sacramenti*), for that is what they are the sign of; but by '*real accompaniment*' (*reali concomitantia*) beneath the appearances of wine, because his body goes with his blood in reality. What is not separate in reality is not separate in the sacrament. So what exists together in reality is also found altogether under either sign.[110] Christ's body can no more be separated from his blood now than Shylock could have had a pound of Antonio's flesh without a drop of his blood. Conversely, Christ's blood is present beneath the appearances of wine 'by the power of the sacrament', for these are the sacramental sign of his blood; and 'by real accompaniment' beneath the appearances of bread, as his blood goes with his body in reality.[111] What is present by the power of the sacrament is what the sign signifies. What is present by real accompaniment is what goes in reality with the thing (body or blood) present by the power of the sacrament. Thus the whole Christ is present under either *species*.

As Christ's body is not separate from his soul, and his human nature remains for ever united to his divine nature, we receive the whole Christ, 'body, blood, soul and divinity', under either species (kind). Christ's divinity is present by the hypostatic union, that is, by the union of his human to divine nature in his person. Thus we receive a share in Christ's divinity through his humanity. 'The whole Christ exists in this sacrament', St Thomas says. And this for two reasons: (1) because his body and soul were rejoined at his resurrection, and (2) because Christ is present 'by way of substance', which is whole in every part. The Eucharist is itself evidence for the resurrection of Christ's body, because we could not now have a sacrament of his *life-giving* body and blood unless his body had been raised up to life again. Although the Eucharist

110. ST 76,1.
111. ST 76,2.

is the commemoration of Christ's passion, St Thomas states clearly that his *risen* body is present in the Eucharist, as it truly is now. But this does not prevent the Eucharist from representing Christ's passion, because his risen body still bears the marks of his passion in his now glorious wounds.

As the whole Christ is present beneath either sacramental appearance, when the host is broken Christ's body itself is not broken or divided, but only the sacramental appearances are broken.[112] As St Thomas nicely expresses it in the sequence for Corpus Christi, *Lauda, Sion*:

> *Nulla rei fit scissura,*
> *Signi tantum fit fractura.*

Literally, there is no cutting of the reality, only the breaking of the sign. As the breaking of the host only affects the sign, so likewise we do not bite Christ's body itself with our teeth but eat him beneath sacramental appearances. Thus St Thomas strikes a balance between what to some seemed the too physical view of Paschasius and a purely spiritual view of the Eucharist, which could always find support in St Augustine. Christ is as present in every particle of a host as he is in a whole host. Christ is present in every fragment, St Thomas says, 'as visual appearances are multiplied in a thousand mirrors.'[113] Many mirrors reflect one and the same complete image of the sun as one mirror does. St Thomas makes it clear that to eat Christ 'spiritually' in the Eucharist means to eat him with charity and in the unity of the Church. 'He spiritually eats Christ's body and blood who participates in the unity of the Church, which is brought about by charity.'[114]

The Eucharist is in several ways 'the sacrament of truth'. First, it contains Christ himself, who is 'full of grace and truth' (Jn 1, 14). Secondly, there is no deception in this sacrament: the eye is not

---

112. ST 3a 77, 7 ad 3.
113. *Sermon on the Body of the Lord.*
114. *Super Ioannem* VI lect. 6.

deceived by what it sees, for the appearances of bread and wine are just what they appear to be – appearances. Thirdly, Christ's body and blood are present in this sacrament in truth (*in veritate*); it is not a figure of them. Fourthly, we can trust the words of consecration: "This is my body", "This is the cup of my blood", because they are the words of Christ who is the Truth himself. St Cyril of Alexandria says, 'The truth does not lie.'[115] And as Aquinas himself says in the *Adoro te devote*:

Nil hoc verbo veritatis verius.

Literally, there is nothing more true than this word of the Truth. Or, in the rendering of Gerard Manley Hopkins (Godhead here in hiding):

Truth speaks truly or there is nothing true.

The Council of Trent

The first attacks on the doctrine of transubstantiation at the Reformation were already sounded over 100 years earlier, in the late fourteenth century. Although John Wyclif (c. 1330-1384) held the Church's belief for most of his life, he began to doubt it around 1380 and then rejected transubstantiation, because the idea that accidents could exist without their substance seemed to him absurd. His reason for raising this objection may not, however, have been so much on philosophical grounds as polemic, in order to ridicule the belief of priests whom he wanted to attack for their moral failings and clerical abuses (the system of taking stipends). He claimed that transubstantiation was not supported by Scripture, and came to believe that the proper words should be "This bread is my body", because to say "This is my body" looks like the tautology of saying "This body is my body." He thus adopted a belief close to consubstantiation: bread and wine remain, because they are not annihilated. Luther took up a similar position.

---

115. Quoted by St Thomas, ST 3a 75,1.

Wyclif did not deny the Real Presence but said that Christ is 'spiritually' present. We can trace a direct line of descent of thought from Ratramnus and Berengar through Wyclif to Luther and the Reformers.

The Reformers chiefly directed their attacks on the Eucharist against two doctrines: transubstantiation and the sacrifice of the Mass. They were divided among themselves in their attack on the Church. The differences between the chief Reformers can be simply given as follows:

Luther took the position that Christ is truly present, but 'in, with and under' bread and wine. This is the doctrine of consubstantiation, that Christ is present besides bread and wine, which are not changed but remain.

Melancthon, Luther's right hand man, primarily saw the Eucharist as a banquet to be eaten. Thus he taught that Christ is not present in the Eucharist outside its actual celebration. He consequently rejected reservation and adoration of the Blessed Sacrament outside Mass.

Zwingli, the extreme Swiss Reformer, held that Christ's body cannot be in the sacrament, as it is in heaven. Christ is only present in the soul of believers through faith. The Eucharist is a mere memorial of the Last Supper.

Calvin adopted a view between Luther's and Zwingli's. With Zwingli, he held that Christ's body is in heaven but thought that it can be linked to signs in virtue of the power of the Holy Spirit. Unlike Zwingli, however, he added that truth is joined to the signs of the sacrament.

Common to Melancthon and Zwingli is denial that the Mass is a sacrifice: for Melancthon it is just a banquet, for Zwingli just a memorial.

In answering the Reformers, the Council of Trent, at its Thirteenth Session in October 1551, under Pope Julius III, said that the change of bread and wine in the Eucharist is 'substantial' and this change is, therefore, most fittingly called 'transubstantiation', because it is one of substance.

> It has ever been a firm belief of the Church of God ... that through the consecration of the bread and wine a conversion is made of the whole substance of the bread into the substance of the body of Christ our Lord, and of the whole substance of wine into the substance of his blood. This conversion is suitably and properly called by the Catholic Church, transubstantiation.[116]

We may note that the phrase, 'the whole substance of bread is converted into the substance of the body of Christ, and the whole substance of wine into the substance of the blood of Christ' comes from St Thomas.[117]

In the canons attached to this decree, Trent said:

> If anyone denies the wonderful and singular conversion of the whole substance of the bread into the body, and of the whole substance of the wine into the blood, only the *species* of bread and wine remaining, which conversion the Catholic Church indeed aptly calls transubstantiation, let him be accursed (*anathema sit*).[118]

The question is whether transubstantiation is *de fide*, that is, something that Catholics have to believe. Is it part of Trent's *definition* of the Eucharist as the body and blood of Christ? Some maintain that the word 'transubstantiation' is not part of the definition itself. Even when we grant this view, however, that it does not belong to the definition, what is quite clear from the wording is that the content of the belief that is 'properly and suitably called transubstantiation', namely the change of the substance of bread

---

116. *Decree on the Most Holy Eucharist* c. 4, ND 1519.
117. ST 3a 75, 4c.
118. Canon 2, ND 1527.

and wine into the body and blood of Christ, *is* something that Catholics have to believe. So even if Catholics do not have to believe in transubstantiation itself, they have to affirm the content of the doctrine that is aptly called 'transubstantiation'. Thus they *virtually* believe in transubstantiation if they accept the doctrine that was defined by the Council of Trent. When we want to know what it is we are required to believe by the Church, a sure guide is to look at the canons attached to a decree rather than the text of the decree itself. Moloney says that Canon 2 deals with an article of faith.[119] This canon was directed against Luther's alternative of consubstantiation. It says that you cannot have the real presence of Christ in the Eucharist without a substantial change of bread and wine. (Luther thought that Christ was present with bread and wine.)

Although it is common for people to think that the idea of transubstantiation depends on Aristotle's philosophy of substance and accidents, and consequently we do not have to accept it, because the Church never ties her teachings to a particular philosophy, it is possible to show that this objection is historically false. First, 'transubstantiation' is the word for a change of substance, just as 'transformation' is the natural word for a change of form. But the Church already spoke about a change of substance in the Eucharist when she said bread and wine are 'substantially converted' in 1079. No one suggests that the philosophy of Aristotle was being used by the Church at that time, because it only entered into theology at Paris at the beginning of the thirteenth century, which was 150 years later. So the change of substance was not a particularly Aristotelian doctrine. As already noted, 'substance' was first used to exclude 'figure'. The word 'transubstantiate' was first used by the Church at the Fourth Lateran Council, in 1215, when she said that bread and wine are 'transubstantiated'. This was ten years before St Thomas was born.

---

119. *The Eucharist*, p. 165.

When Aquinas came to explain how Christ comes to be *really* present in the Eucharist by a change of the substance of bread and wine into his body and blood, he was only taking up the way the Church had already begun to express her faith in the Eucharist. Of course he found in Aristotle's philosophy of substance a ready tool at hand for reflecting on what the Church meant by 'substantial conversion'. St Thomas, however, said himself that he learnt more in prayer than he ever did from books. The primary source of St Thomas' theology of the Eucharist, then, is not to be sought in the philosophy of Aristotle but in his own devotion to Christ in the Eucharist. Whether we are attracted by his approach or not, it found expression in the devotional hymns that he wrote for the feast of Corpus Christi and which remain until today a fruitful source of devotion in parishes everywhere. As Colman O'Neill observes, the dogmatic formula of substantial change and 'transubstantiated' existed in the Church before Aquinas' theological explanation of them.

The objection that transubstantiation depends on the philosophy of Aristotle can be shown to be untrue. For the Council of Trent did not contrast substance with accidents, as Aristotle did, but with *species* (appearances). In preferring 'appearances' to 'accidents', Trent took up a word that had been used earlier in the Church's tradition by the Fathers. O'Neill says that no-one today seriously maintains that Trent incorporated scholastic theology into the Church's dogma of the Eucharist.[120] He says that we need not attach any more specific meaning to the terms used at the Council of Trent than they possess in their pre-philosophic usage. He does not think that we are required to understand 'substance' as used in the decree of Trent in any other way than in its ordinary 'common-sense' notion.[121] He writes:

> Along the lines of the common-sense interpretation here proposed the "dogma of transubstantiation" presents no

---

120. *New Approaches*, p. 77.
121. Ibid., p. 78.

very complicated concept. It simply states in pre-philo-sophic terms, what must be postulated if Christ's words *This is my body, my blood* are to be verified by faith: namely, the whole substance of the bread must be changed into Christ's body, the whole substance of wine into his blood. What the dogma states is no more than what is required if Christ's words, as spoken at the Last Supper and at Mass, are to be understood as referring to the thing placed on the table or contained in the cup. For, at the pre-philosophical level of common-sense, "substance" is that which permits us to say that a thing existing independently of ourselves, our knowledge or our attitudes, is either bread or the body of Christ. And it is apparent to common-sense that a thing understood in this way may not be simultaneously bread and the body of Christ.[122]

O'Neill maintains that the Church uses the word 'substance' for the Eucharist, because she upholds the independent reality of things; we are not confined to merely subjective knowledge of things. 'Substance' means that things have an independent exist-ence in themselves; they have their own characteristics and are not just what they are for me. After the consecration, the things placed on the altar are the body and blood of Christ: 'In common-sense terms this involves a substantial change in bread and wine; and this is transubstantiation.'[123] O'Neill is supported by his fellow Irish Dominican, Bishop William Barden OP: 'the Catholic dogma defined at the Council of Trent teaches that the substance of bread does not remain but is changed into the body of Christ – *transubstantiation.*'[124] As O'Neill indicates, by speaking of a substantial change we secure the truth that the Eucharist cannot *really* be both bread and the body of Christ at the same time: it can

---

122. Ibid., p. 86.
123. Ibid., p. 89.
124. *Summa* vol. 58, n 59 (Barden's italics).

only really be one *or* the other – bread and wine or the body and blood of Christ. Moloney agrees with O'Neill when he sees in the miracle of Cana a foreshadowing of the change that occurs in the Eucharist: we grasp, he says, that in the change of water and wine there is a change of substance.[125] He too agrees that 'substance' belongs to the ordinary language of common-sense.

O'Neill was only making the same point as Paul VI had in his encyclical, *Mysterium Fidei*, published in 1965 as a response to the theory of transignification. There Paul VI spoke of certain words which are intelligible to all peoples in every age, because they arise from common human experience, and named 'substance' as one of these words.

> These formulas, and others too which the Church employs in proposing dogmas of faith, express concepts which are not tied to any specific cultural system ... They present the perception which the human mind acquires from its universal, essential experience of reality ... They are, therefore, within the reach of everyone at all times and in all places.[126]

With the support of texts from the Fathers, Paul VI demonstrates that the appearances of the sacrament contain a new reality.[127] Quoting St Ambrose, he ascribes the change to the creative action of God: the power which effects the change 'is the same as that by which almighty God created all things from nothing at the beginning of time.'[128]

It is noteworthy that Paul VI thought it fitting to include special mention of transubstantiation in his concise summary of the Faith, *'The Credo of the People of God'* (1968): 'This hidden conversion is appropriately and justly called by the Church

---

125. Op. cit., p. 163.
126. *Mysterium Fidei* 24.
127. Ibid., 47-55.
128. Ibid., 51.

transubstantiation.'[129] It seems to be the present mind of the Church that we retain this doctrine, for we find the word embedded in the section on the Real Presence in the *Catechism of the Catholic Church*, which says 'Trent summarises catholic faith on this point' (the conversion of bread and wine into the body and blood of Christ), quotes c. 4 of the decree of Trent, and ends with the word 'transubstantiation', which is emphasised in the English version.[130]

We now turn to the theory of transignification, with which several writers sought to replace the doctrine of a change of substance in the middle of the twentieth century.

Transignification

We have already noted that what is on the altar after the consecration does not just signify Christ's flesh but *is* Christ's flesh. There is an identify of the reality of the sacrament, 'the real thing', with Christ's body and blood. This understanding of the Eucharist was called into question by the theory of transignification in the 1940s. The pioneer of this theory was Père Yves de Montcheuil (d. 1944) with his book *La Présence Réelle*. He was followed by the Frenchman De Baciocchi among others. Transignification is the theory that things are what we mean them to be for us or what we use them for. Thus silver becomes money when we use it in exchange for buying things. A piece of paper that can be used as money is not just paper but a bank note. Nevertheless a bank note remains paper, and a silver coin remains silver, even though they have received a new use. In the same way, the theory of transignification said that bread becomes the body of Christ when we use it in the Eucharist for a spiritual purpose. This theory, however, is inadequate, because it would mean that bread and wine were not *really* the body and blood of Christ but remained bread and wine; they would not be *changed* but only receive a new use.

---

129. CTS translation, p. 12.
130. CCC 1376 (ND 1519).

Criticism of the doctrine of transubstantiation sprang from two sources. First, empirical science seemingly rendered the word 'substance' meaningless, because it could no longer be applied to matter as modern physics showed it to be. For instance, it is not possible to ascertain any chemical change of the constitution of bread and wine in the Eucharist. Karl Rahner echoes this sort of criticism of calling bread a substance at all when he follows the view that it is just an 'agglomeration of substances.' This ignores what people commonly recognise: that bread has its own identity, and there is something that it is *as a whole*. It is not just a collection of ingredients without any unity. Quantum physics' view of matter is just as questionable as Aristotle's view of substance. Scientists overlook that objects have a unity, though consisting of innumerable particles, and that there is something they are *as wholes*. A human being, for example, is not just a mass of atoms consisting of particles in motion. We can say *what* a thing is as a whole; for example, bread, or wine, or a lemon, or linen. It was for these everyday purposes that Aristotle used the word substance. Moloney remarks that questions about atoms and particles are misplaced with regard to the Eucharist. But he seems to miss the point about the change of substance in the Eucharist when he says that 'there will always have to be some substantial form or forms, of whatever kind, giving reality to the physical entities.'[131] For this is just the point: bread and wine do not receive the form of Christ; the physical entities in the Eucharist do not have a *substantial* form of their own, for bread and wine no longer remain but only their appearances, or accidents, do. They *are* the body and blood of Christ.

The second source of criticism of transubstantiation in the middle of the twentieth century was existential philosophy. Scholastic theology ceased to be meaningful for many who regarded existentialism and phenomenology as more relevant philosophies for

131. Op. cit., pp. 180 f.

human life. Heidegger, for instance, observed that many things in the world do not just exist but exist in relation *to us* as we use them for various purposes. This is especially true of objects in the house. But things have their own identity and nature. It is a kind of voluntarism to think that things are just what *we* want them to be. They do not just exist for us but in themselves.

A kind of scepticism also prevailed among some, who thought it a vain task to say how Christ is present in the Eucharist. Thus Edward Schillebeeckx OP proposed replacing the old metaphysical approach to the Eucharist with a more anthropological one. A metaphysical approach considers what things are in their own existence; an anthropological one considers things as they are related to us, and persons as related one to another. Metaphysical is about the existence of objects, anthropological is more subjective and primarily about persons. Schillebeeckx himself defines sacraments as 'interpersonal encounters between the believer and Christ.'[132]

According to the theory of transignification, there is a change of meaning, not of substance, in the Eucharist. Bread is not itself changed but it signifies something new. Bread and wine acquire a new meaning when the words of consecration are spoken over them. This theory proposes that there is not a change of what is really there but only of its purpose and use: bread and wine are no longer ordinary food and drink but express friendship with Christ. The background of this theory is the use of the continental philosophy of phenomenology in theology. Phenomenology says that things consist of the appearances. This philosophy does not so much consider what things are in themselves but what they are *for me*. Thus things are not seen as independent realities but in relation to human beings. *Gaudium et Spes* comments on this view: the reality of a thing is not only what it means for us; things have their own truth and goodness.[133] Other writers, coming

---

132. *The Eucharist* (1968) p. 101.
133. GS 36.

from phenomenology, observed that human beings are by nature makers of symbols and communicate through symbols. So they saw bread and wine merely as symbols in the Eucharist (they did not say that they are changed altogether). Moloney comments on these theories, that a change of meaning is only a *mental* change, not a real one: it is a change of the way we regard something, not of the thing itself.[134]

In the new theory, presence means the presence of one *person* to another; so Christ's presence in the Eucharist does not require a change of the reality of bread and wine. The important thing, on this view, is that the *person* of Christ is present to the believer. This overlooks the truth that Christ's flesh and blood are the source of divine life for us in the Eucharist because they are really present. The view that the primary thing is the relation of Christ to the believer, not what the sacrament is in *itself*, resembles views of the Reformers that Christ is present to those who receive communion by faith. This makes Christ's presence in the Eucharist depend on our faith, not on the power of his words spoken at the consecration.

Schillebeeckx argues that a change of being comes about through a change of meaning. The deepest level of reality, he says, resides in the meaning of a thing: the role it plays in our life. He takes the example of an ancient temple that is now in ruins, visited by modern tourists. He observes it has a different meaning for tourists now than it did for worshippers in ancient times, but he omits to say that the temple still consists of stones as it did then, although it has lost its original meaning.[135] It is still a temple, though a ruined one; that is why tourists visit it. It is just at this level, of *what* the thing is, that a change occurs in the Eucharist; not just of the use of the bread but of the bread itself.

Schillebeeckx is surely wrong to claim that Aquinas situates the saving power of the sacrament in the real presence of Christ

---

134. Op. cit., p. 184.
135. *The Eucharist*, p. 113.

in the community rather than in the sacrament itself.[136] He cites *Summa* 3a 73, 1 and 73, 3. What Aquinas says is that there can be no salvation without the Church.[137] This is not the same as saying that Christ's real presence is in the Church rather than in the Eucharist. St Thomas explicitly says that the *sacrament* has Christ, not the community.[138] If only Christ's saving power, and not Christ himself, is present in the Eucharist, the Eucharist does not differ from the other sacraments. Likewise, Aquinas says that 'the sacrament and reality' (*sacramentum et res*) reside in the matter of the sacrament itself, not just in believers. It is true, however, that there is no salvation without the reality of the sacrament (*res sacramenti*), which is the unity of Christ's mystical body, the Church. Schillebeeckx, however, professes that he could not rest content with a purely phenomenological approach to the Eucharist, in which things have no reality independent of the perceiver or believer.[139]

The Dutch Capuchin father, Luchesius Smits, held that there is a change of sign, not of substance. It has already been pointed out that bread and wine are not anyway the signs of this sacrament, but their *appearances* are. Smits' theory was that, since Christ as man expressed his love for his disciples symbolically in bread and wine at the Last Supper, so they become the medium of the meeting of friends at a new, deeper level in Mass. As Christ is not only man but God as well, bread and wine now signify the love of one who is both God and man for us, and thus they mediate our meeting with someone who is divine.

The theory of transignification may be criticised under the following six points:

1. If the Eucharist is merely a symbol, it is distinguished too little from the other sacraments.

---

136. Ibid., p. 110.
137. Ibid., 73, 3.
138. Ibid., 73, 1 ad 3.
139. *The Eucharist*, p. 149.

2. Transignification focuses on what things are for me but not on the words of consecration and what they *do* (God's word is *active* and effective).

3. Aidan Nichols makes two points:

(a). God's creative activity touches bread and wine, totally changing them.

(b). Individual things have an independent existence in themselves, not only in relation to me. The same point is also made by O'Neill.[140] Christ's real presence is also a personal presence.

4. Both Nichols and O'Neill find that transignification says too little about the *sacrifice* of the Mass. The theory hardly touches it, and only accounts for communion.[141] Christ offers himself to the Father, not just to us in communion. So one criterion for a true doctrine of Christ's presence in the Eucharist is whether it also allows that Christ offers himself in it. Those who attacked the Real Presence at the Reformation also denied that the Mass is a sacrifice. The symbolism of the Mass is that Christ gave himself to us at the Last Supper precisely to be offered by us.[142]

5. O'Neill points out, against Smits, that Christ did not simply establish a means of expressing his friendship with his disciples at the Last Supper, but did it in a particular way, namely by offering his life for us as a sacrifice for sin. The words of consecration themselves refer to the sacrifice: "given up for you", "poured out for many."

6. Paul VI was able to turn the scales against the proponents of transignification by pointing out that bread and wine only acquire a new meaning in the Eucharist *because* they are changed into a new reality. The new meaning depends

---

140. *New Approaches*, p. 85.
141. Nichols, p. 116.
142. O'Neill, p. 108.

on the change of bread and wine. 'But if they acquire a new significance and a new finality, it is because they contain a new reality, which we justly call ontological.'[143] ('Ontological' means 'of the being of a thing'.) Pope Paul VI went so far as to say that Christ's body is physically present in the Eucharist: 'Beneath these appearances, Christ is present whole and entire, bodily present too, in his physical reality, although not in the manner bodies are present in place.'[144] He did this, to affirm unequivocally the reality of Christ's presence in the Eucharist. The Real Presence means that the Eucharist contains an objective reality after the consecration, which exists independently of our minds.

Transignification, then, brings us back to the Real Presence. It also shows us that when we alter the doctrine of Christ's presence in the Eucharist we lose the view of it as a sacrifice. So we now turn to the sacrifice in the Mass and its relation to the Real Presence.

---

143. *Mysterium Fidei* 46.
144. Ibid., 46.

Chapter 4

The Sacrifice of the Mass

In the previous chapter, we discussed the Real Presence; how the gifts of bread and wine are changed into the body and blood of Christ. In this chapter we shall consider how the body and blood of Christ are then offered to the Father in sacrifice. When Christ took bread at the Last Supper and said "This is my body", and took the cup of blessing and said "This is the cup of my blood", he did this as a sign of the sacrifice of his own life which he was about to offer to the Father the next day, to atone for the sins of the world. Thus there is a close connection between the two main aspects of the Eucharist: the presence of Christ's real body and blood, and the sacrifice of them. In communion he gives us his body and blood, which he gave up for us on the cross when he offered himself up to his Father for our sakes. 'Christ gives us the very body he gave up on the cross, the blood he shed for many for the forgiveness of sins.'[145] That the Mass is a sacrifice depends on the words of consecration, for what is offered after the conse-cration is not bread and wine but the body and blood of Christ. After seeing how the Mass is a sacrifice, we shall return to the connection of the two main aspects of the Eucharist at the end of this chapter. St Thomas said that the Eucharist is a sacrifice as it is offered, and a sacrament as it is received.[146] He saw the two chief figures of this in the Old Testament in the Passover Lamb, as it is offered, and the manna (bread from heaven), as it is eaten.

The Mass is not only a sacrament but also a sacrifice. Indeed Christ instituted the Eucharist at the Last Supper as a sign of the

---

145. CCC 1365.
146. ST 3a 79,5.

sacrifice he was to offer the following day on the cross. 'Our Saviour instituted the Eucharistic sacrifice of his body and blood. He did this in order to perpetuate the sacrifice of the cross throughout the centuries until he should come again.'[147] The Mass has a past aspect, the memorial of Christ's passion; and a future aspect – we perpetuate this memorial until Christ's Second Coming at the end of time. These two aspects are closely related, for the means by which we *look forward* in hope to Christ's Second Coming is precisely by recalling his Death and Resurrection in the past. This is neatly summed up for us by St Paul: 'You shall proclaim the death of the Lord until he comes' (1 Cor 11:26). We do not, however, just proclaim the Lord's death but his sacrifice is also made *present* in the Mass.[148] Fr James O'Connor says: 'This memorial is not a mere figure but brings about what it signifies. The once-and-for-all sacrifice of the Lord is made effectively present in the sacrifice of the Mass.'[149]

To make present again is, literally, to *re-present*. Thus St Thomas calls the Eucharist an *imago representativa* (a representing image) of Christ's passion, which he says was a true immolation.[150] The Mass is an 'image' of the passion, because sacraments not only signify by their words but also their *actions*. The Eucharist is a re-enactment of the passion, when Christ's blood was separated from his body, but in a different way from a play on the stage. For example, Shakespeare's play *Henry V* does not make present again the Battle of Agincourt as the Mass makes present for us Christ's sacrifice on the cross. For one thing, Henry V is not really present on the stage as Christ is in the Eucharist. Thus the sacrifice of the Mass depends on the Real Presence. If Christ were not *really* present in the Eucharist, it would not be a sacrifice. When Reformers denied the Real Presence in the 16th century, it was

147. SC 47.
148. *New Approaches*, p. 16.
149. *The Hidden Manna*, p. 245.
150. ST 3a 83,1.

only consistent of them to reject the Mass as a sacrifice; for they perceived that the second is only given with the first. The Mass does not just proclaim the Lord's death but also makes it present again, because the very same thing, or victim, is offered to the Father in the Mass as was offered on the cross: namely, Christ's body and blood. The prayers of the Mass indicate that the proper offering occurs *after* the consecration: for example, 'We offer you in thanksgiving this holy and living sacrifice'[151] and 'we offer you his body and blood, the acceptable sacrifice which brings salvation to the whole world.'[152]

Before we look at the relation of the Mass to the sacrifice of the cross, we shall first briefly notice the basis of the Church's doctrine in the early tradition and Fathers of the Church. For its foundation in the New Testament, look back to chapter one, especially in the section on the New Covenant.

To set this chapter in clearer perspective, it will help us first to recall that, according to Aquinas, all the sacraments derive their power from the cross and apply its saving power, but especially the Eucharist. For they do for us what Christ did on the cross: they free us from sin and perfect us for the worship of God. The perfect act of worship was the sacrifice Christ offered in obedience on the cross. So the Mass is now the perfect act of worship and the centre of all that the Church does. St Thomas says that in offering himself as an oblation and victim to God,[153] Christ freed us from sin and initiated the rite of Christian worship.[154] Aquinas sees the sign of this in the blood and water which flowed from Christ's side on the cross.[155] The water and blood symbolised the two chief sacraments of Christian worship: Baptism and the Eucharist respectively.

---

151. Eucharistic Prayer III.
152. Eucharistic Prayer IV.
153. Eph 5:2.
154. ST 3a 62,5.
155. Jn 19:34.

The Fathers on Sacrifice

From very early the Church saw the Eucharist as the fulfilment of the prophecy of Malachi that a pure sacrifice would be offered in every place and every time: 'From the rising of the sun to its setting a pure offering is offered to my name'(1:11). This text is quoted by the *Didache* (end of first century), which calls the Eucharist the *thusia* (sacrifice) of Christians.[156] They saw that the Eucharist supersedes the sacrifices of the Old Testament as the Church's principal act of worship.

The Eucharist was a sacrifice for Justin,[157] and for Irenaeus it was 'the new oblation of the New Covenant'.[158] The sacrifice on earth participates in the heavenly sacrifice.[159]

St Cyprian, writing in Northern Africa in the middle of the third century, sees a direct relation between the Eucharist and the cross: 'The passion of the Lord is the sacrifice we offer.'[160]

St Gregory Nazianzen, in the fourth century, is the first to state the view that the Eucharist is a sacramental sacrifice, because the bread and wine are consecrated separately, just as Christ's blood was separated from his body in his passion.[161]

St Cyril of Jerusalem calls the Eucharist 'a spiritual sacrifice', in which Christ, 'the victim of propitiation', is present: 'we offer Christ sacrificed for our sins.'[162] Thus Cyril states explicitly that the Mass is *propitiatory*, offered for the forgiveness of sins.

St Ambrose makes the point, that it is *Christ* who really offers the sacrifice of the Mass.[163]

St John Chrysostom anticipated the medieval theory of the

---

156. *Did.* 14.
157. *Dialogue* 70.
158. *Adversus Haereses* IV 17,5.
159. Ibid., IV 18.
160. *Epistola 63*, 17.
161. *Epist. 171*.
162. *Myst. Cat. 5,8-18*, quoted in *Mysterium Fidei* 30.
163. *Expos. in Ps. 38*, PL 1051-52.

sacrifice of the Mass with this classic passage, cited by Aquinas, who wrongly attributed it to Ambrose.[164]

> Do we carry out an oblation every day? We do indeed, but by carrying out the commemoration (*anamnesis*) of his death, and this commemoration is one, not several. How one and not several? Because he was offered up once only, like the offering in the Holy of Holies. The one is the type of the other, and so is the Eucharist also. We are always offering the same victim, not one sheep today and another tomorrow, but always the same one, so that the sacrifice is one ... But everywhere there is one Christ, as complete in one place as in another, one body. Therefore as he who is offered up in many places is one body and not many bodies, so it is one sacrifice. He is our High Priest who offered up the sacrifice which purifies us ... This comes about by the commemoration of what once took place, for he says: "Do this in commemoration of me".[165]

The many sacrifices of the Old Testament are replaced by one and the same sacrifice which is always offered in the new and everlasting covenant. Chrysostom argues that the Eucharist is the same sacrifice as the cross, because the same Christ is present in the Eucharist. The identity of the sacrifice in the Eucharist with that on the cross follows from the real presence of Christ. 'The death of Christ is carried out, the awesome sacrifice' in the Eucharist.[166] Like Irenaeus, Chrysostom too says that the offering on earth is taken up to share in the heavenly sacrifice.[167]

Theodoret of Cyrus (c. 393-460) repeats this point, that it is the *same* sacrifice, when he asks why the priests of the New Covenant continually celebrate the mystic liturgy if Christ's once-and-for-all

---

164. ST 3a 83,1.
165. *Hom. in Hebr.* 17,3.
166. *Hom. in Acta* 21,4.
167. *Hom. in Hebr.* 11,2-3.

sacrifice is supposed to be all-sufficient? If it is truly sufficient to take away the sins of all time, surely we would not need to offer sacrifice any more after the cross. Theodoret replies: 'It is plain to all those versed in divine things that we do not offer another sacrifice, but ours recalls the one saving sacrifice.'[168]

But the chief Patristic source for the doctrine of the sacrifice of the Mass in the West is St Augustine in the *City of God*, book X. He exhorts those who join in offering the public sacrifice also to make an interior sacrifice of their own lives.

> When we lift up our hearts to him, our heart is his altar. We propitiate him by our priest, his only-begotten Son. We sacrifice blood-stained victims to him when we fight for truth "as far as shedding our blood".[169]

Further on, Augustine defines a sacrifice thus:

> A sacrifice is a divine matter; something is not a sacrifice unless it is done for the sake of God.

> The whole redeemed community, that is to say, the congregation and fellowship of saints, is offered to God as a universal sacrifice, through the Great High Priest who offered himself in suffering for us, so that we might be the body of so great a head.[170]

The Church not only offers the sacrifice of the Eucharist but is herself offered in the very sacrifice she herself offers, because the Head and the body make the *whole* Christ. The Eucharist is given as a sign, St Augustine says, that in the sacrifice she offers the Church is offered too:

> This is the sacrifice which the Church continually celebrates in the sacrament of the altar, a sacrament well known to the faithful, where it is shown to the Church

168. *Comm. in Hebr.* 8,4.
169. *City of God* X c. 3.
170. Ibid., X c. 6.

that she herself is offered in the offering which she presents to God.[171]

The key to Augustine's doctrine of the sacrifice of the Eucharist is the *unity* of the body of Christ with the Head. Christ is himself the sacrifice as well as the one who offers it: he is the priest and oblation in one. As the Church is his body, she is offered in offering it. Christ also receives the Church's (that is, our) offering and unites it with his offering of himself to the Father.

> Thus he is both the priest, himself making the offering, and the oblation. This is the reality, and he intended the daily sacrifice of the Church to be the sacramental symbol of this; for the Church, being the body of which he is the Head, learns to offer herself through him. This is the true sacrifice; and the sacrifices of the saints in earlier times were many different symbols of it.[172]

Thus Augustine sees the relation of the Eucharist to the sacrifice of the cross as that of a sacramental symbol. Christ's death on the cross was a sacrifice, because he *voluntarily* offered up his life to his Father. *He* offered himself, his slayers did not offer him; so offerer and victim are one and the same.[173]

The Same Sacrifice

The Council of Trent gave three reasons why the Mass is a sacrifice:

1. Because it represents the sacrifice of the cross.

2. It is the memorial of the cross.

3. It applies the fruits of the Passion to individuals.[174]

This third reason is what we mean by saying that the Mass is *propitiatory.*

---

171. Ibid., X c. 6.
172. Ibid., X c. 20.
173. Aquinas, ST 3a 48,3 ad 3.
174. ND 1546, quoted in CCC 1366.

The Mass represents the sacrifice of the cross (it is an *imago representativa*) particularly at two points in its action: at the consecration by the separate consecration of bread and wine, and at the fraction of the host just before communion. These are the signs of the passion of Christ's body, St Thomas says.[175] Thus the immolation of the victim in the Mass is *sacramental*, that is, it is represented by signs. (To immolate is to kill a victim as a sacrifice.) The Council of Trent said: 'At the Last Supper Christ left the Church a *visible* sacrifice, by which the bloody sacrifice to be accomplished once for all on the cross might be represented.'[176] The Cross and the Mass are *one single sacrifice*, because the victim and offerer in both are the same.[177] The Mass and the Cross differ solely in the manner of offering the sacrifice: on the Cross it was in a bloody manner, in the Mass in an *unbloody* way. 'In this divine sacrifice, which is carried out in the Mass, the same Christ is contained and unbloodily immolated, who "offered himself once for all" (Heb 9:14) bloodily on the altar of the cross.'[178] Or, as Cardinal Cajetan put it, 'The sacrifice was then offered in a material way, now it is offered in a spiritual manner.' Thus the Mass is a spiritual sacrifice, as it says in Hebrews 9:14: 'how much more shall the blood of Christ, who through the eternal Spirit offered himself without blemish to the Father, purify your conscience from dead works to serve the living God.' One reason why the only true sacrifice that can be offered after the Cross is an unbloody one is that Christ rose, *'never to die again'* (Rom 6:9). So there is no more slaying of victims or of the victim, but only the offering of the same perfect victim who was once slain but now lives for ever. Thus the passion of Christ is not 'itself present in the Mass but Christ who suffered (*Christus passus*) is present.'[179] St Thomas quotes Rev 5:6:

---

175. ST 3a 76,2 ad 1: 77,7.
176. 22nd session, c. 1.
177. ND 1548, CCC 1367.
178. Trent XXII c. 2 (DS 1743).
179. ST 3a 83,1.

'I saw a Lamb standing, as though it had been slain.'[180] Although Christ is really present in the Mass as he is *now*, glorified in heaven, the glorified Christ is the Christ who suffered and still bears the marks of his glorious wounds. 'The Eucharist is the perfect sacrament of the Lord's passion, since it contains Christ who has suffered.'[181]

The third respect in which the Mass is a sacrifice is that it applies the fruits of Christ's passion to individuals. 'By this sacrament we are made participants of the fruit of the Lord's passion.'[182] In the same article, St Thomas also argues the other way round: as we receive the fruits of redemption through the Eucharist, so it must be a sacrifice. As the effect of this sacrament is to share in the fruit of the Lord's passion, 'it is proper to this sacrament that Christ is immolated in its celebration.'[183]

Since Christ's sacrifice of himself, the perfect victim, completed and superseded all the sacrifices of the Old Testament, the Mass now remains the only true sacrifice to be offered on Earth, as it represents Christ's sacrifice on the Cross. As all the sacrifices of the Old Testament prefigured Christ's sacrifice, so it can be said that Christ was immolated in them. Not only is his sacrifice perpetual, for eternity, but it also reaches back in time: Christ is 'the Lamb who has been slain since the origin of the world'(Rev 13:8). The sacrifices of the Old Law contained the true sacrifice of Christ in a symbol, but the sacrifice of the New Law contains Christ in reality.[184]

This sacrifice has been offered since the foundation of the world, in the sacrifices that prefigured it until Christ came, and it will go on being offered until the end of time, 'until he comes again.' The passion of Christ goes on until the end of the world,

---

180. Ibid., 83,1 ad 2.
181. ST 73,5 ad 2.
182. ST 3a 83,1.
183. ST 83,1.
184. ST 3a 73,4 ad 3.

says St Leo the Great.[185] It is a perpetual sacrifice that continues to be offered in heaven, because Christ's attitude of obedience to his Father is permanent in heaven. The letter to the Hebrews 10:5-10 argues that Christ's sacrifice was primarily one of his own will, in fulfilment of Psalm 38 (39):6-8:

> Behold, I have come to do your will.

Christ continues to plead for us before his Father in heaven with the body he offered on the cross and took up to the true sanctuary in heaven at his Ascension.[186] This is the body that is really present and offered to the Father at Mass. Thus the Mass not only commemorates Christ's death and Resurrection but also his Ascension: 'Father, calling to mind the death your Son endured for our salvation, his glorious resurrection and ascension into heaven.'[187] The Mass perpetuates on Earth the eternal sacrifice of the Lamb of God. It is eternal, because our High Priest continually pleads for us before his Father with his wounded human nature, which he took up to heaven to present to the Father.

St John Chrysostom argued that the Eucharist is the same sacrifice as Christ offered on the cross, because Christ speaks the words of consecration through his priest, who consecrates and offers in *persona Christi*:

> 'Even as the words the Lord spoke are the same as the priest says, so too the oblation is identical.'[188]

It is the same oblation because it is offered by the priest, who shares in the priesthood of Christ. 'Christ is the fount of all priesthood.' There is *one* priest, Christ, St Thomas says, and priests share in his one priesthood.[189] Thus there is a close connection between the doctrines of the Eucharist and the priesthood. Indeed the priest

---

185. *Sermo de Passione* 9.
186. Heb 7:25.
187. Eucharistic Prayer III.
188. *In 2 Tim. Hom.* 2,4, quoted in *Mysterium Fidei* 34.
189. ST 3a 22,4.

is for consecrating the Eucharist. It also follows that, as the priest consecrates and offers the Eucharist in *persona Christi*, at this part of the Mass he is not the spokesman of the people but representative of Christ. The priest who offers the sacrifice in the Mass is the same, because the priest at the altar is *Christ's* priest; Christ is represented by his priest.[190] It is the same person now offering the sacrifice at Mass as offered it on the cross.[191]

The Eucharist, however, does not add to Christ's sacrifice as often as it is offered, but makes one and the same sacrifice of the cross present again. To *re-present* is, literally, to make present again. Christ offered this sacrifice once and for all: 'He has no need, like those other priests, to offer sacrifices daily, first for his own sins and then for those of the people; he did this *once for all* when he offered up himself' (Heb 7:27). He could do this 'once for all' because he was without sin and so could offer the *perfect* sacrifice without any blemish. The perfect sacrifice of course completes all other sacrifices and so brings them to an end. After Christ's sacrifice of himself there is no need for any further sacrifices, since none could surpass or even add to his perfect sacrifice. There are not as many sacrifices offered as Masses are said, but *one and the same* sacrifice is offered every time that Mass is said. As Cardinal Journet says, what is renewed is not the bloody sacrifice in an unbloody way, but the exterior rite of the sacrament and the consecration.[192]

Unless the Mass is one and the same sacrifice as Christ offered on the cross, his sacrifice is not the perfect one that fulfils all others, nor is it the once-and-for-all sacrifice.[193] But as it is the perfect sacrifice, we only offer the same sacrifice, for no other sacrifice could add anything to it. If we could add anything to his sacrifice on the cross, then 'Christ died in vain' (Gal 2:21). The Reformers

---

190. Pius XII, *Mediator Dei* 73.
191. Trent, 22nd session c. 2; SC 7.
192. *La Messe. Présence du Sacrifice de la Croix* (1958) p. 359.
193. Heb 7:27, 10:12.

were particularly concerned to uphold this point of St Paul's, lest it seemed that Christ died in vain, but they made a false charge against the Catholic doctrine of the sacrifice of the Mass when they claimed that it was a 'work' which added to Christ's work of Redemption. Although 'the work of our redemption is carried out' (*exercetur*) in the Mass, we do not repeatedly offer Mass as though what Christ did for our redemption were not complete in itself, but because the fruits of Redemption continually need to be applied to individuals in every age. 'As often as the sacrifice of the cross, by which "Christ our Passover is sacrificed" (1 Cor 5:7), is celebrated on the altar, the work of our redemption is carried out.'[194] As Pius XII said, Christ has done enough to save everyone, but he wills the personal co-operation of the faithful in making their own the fruits of redemption he has won for us.[195] In the next paragraph, Pius XII observes that, far from detracting from the value of the cross, the daily continuation of the sacrifice shows more clearly its necessity for us.[196] What Christ did does not need to be completed, but it still needs to be applied to individuals.

To summarise so far. The Mass is a sacrifice, the same sacrifice as Christ offered on the cross, because the same victim is offered in it (Christ's body and blood). The same Christ is offered, as Chrysostom said, but in a different way: then in a bloody way on the cross, now in an unbloody way. This section can best be concluded with the words of the Dominican, Melchior Cano, at the Council of Trent, in 1551 (13th session): the Mass is a sacrifice, because the one who offers it, Christ through the ministry of his priests, is identical with the victim of the cross. Christ alone is the priest, priests offer it in *persona Christi*. We now go on to see how the Mass is at the same time the offering of Christ and of the Church.

---

194. LG 3.
195. *Mediator Dei* 82.
196. Ibid., 83.

Who Offers the Sacrifice?

The sacrifice of Christ is also the sacrifice of the Church. As it says in the *Catechism*, the sacrifice of Christ becomes the sacrifice of the members of his body.[197] This had already been established by St Augustine: in offering Christ to the Father, the Church herself is also offered, for the Head and members together make the whole Christ. The whole Church offers the sacrifice of the Mass, and in offering it she is offered as a whole, for she is the body of Christ.[198] The Mass is 'an act of Christ and his Church', the Second Vatican Council said.[199] Christ associates his members with himself in his own sacrifice.[200] 'In giving his sacrifice to the Church, Christ has also made his own the spiritual sacrifice of the Church, in which she is called to offer herself in union with the sacrifice of Christ.'[201] Then, quoting Vatican II, Pope John Paul II says: 'they (the faithful) offer the divine victim to God and offer themselves along with it.'[202] The priest offers the Eucharistic sacrifice to God in the name of all, and the faithful join in it by virtue of their royal priesthood.[203] The Church makes her own Christ's offering of himself to the Father. We offer to the Father what he has given to us, the gift of his Son. But John Paul II points out that Christ's sacrifice is first a gift offered *to the Father*, and only secondarily is given to us.[204] Head and members are united in offering the Mass. The *whole* Church offers the victim through Christ, because the priest represents the Church, as he acts in *persona Christi* at this point of the Mass.[205] Pope John Paul has said that there is a 'sacramental identification' of the priest

---

197. CCC 1368.
198. *Mysterium Fidei* 31.
199. *Presbyterorum Ordinis* 3, 13.
200. C O'Neill, *New Approaches*, p. 109.
201. *Ecclesia de Eucharistia* 1, 13.
202. Loc. cit., cf. LG 2, 11.
203. Ibid., 3, 28; cf. LG 2, 10.
204. Ibid., 1, 13.
205. Pius XII, *Mediator Dei* 97.

with Christ the High Priest.[206] And Colman O'Neill had earlier said that the priest has the same relation to Christ as the Eucharist has to the Passion; which is that of an image.[207]

The principal offerer of the sacrifice of the Mass, therefore, is Christ, as St Ambrose had said; the faithful offer it through the priest who acts *in persona Christi*, as the Church offers the sacrifice through Christ and with him as he is man. The priest alone brings about the sacrifice, for only the ordained priest has the power to do this; the faithful join in offering it.[208] Henri de Lubac remarks that, as all the faithful share in the priesthood of Christ, they are all members of the one Priest.[209] 'The Eucharist is the effective sign of the spiritual sacrifice offered to God by the whole Church, for the sacrifice of Christians is such that all, in the fullness of their numbers, are one single body in Christ.'[210] As O'Neill remarks, the faithful can offer Christ's sacrifice, because they all make, in the phrase of St Thomas Aquinas, 'as though one mystical person' with him.[211] Not only the priest but the faithful too offer the sacrifice, though in a different way. They offer it through and with the priest: through him as he stands in the person of Christ, and with him as they unite their prayers with his.[212] Fr O'Neill reflects this teaching of Pius XII when he says that the priest alone performs the external rite of offering the sacrifice and the faithful unite their interior sentiments with it. Thus the external rite performed by the priest makes visible the interior worship of the people.[213] A sacrifice is an act of worship. Thus Christ's perfect sacrifice has become the principal act of worship of the Church. Christ's sacrifice on the cross was the external expression of his own interior

---

206. *Ecclesia de Eucharistia* 3, 29.
207. *Meeting Christ in the Sacraments*, p. 223.
208. LG 2, 10.
209. *The Splendour of the Church*, pp. 96-97.
210. J O'Connor, *The Hidden Manna*, p. 245.
211. *Meeting Christ in the Sacraments*, p. 234; cf. ST 3a 48, 2 ad 1.
212. *Mediator Dei* 98.
213. *Meeting Christ in the Sacraments*, p. 232.

dedication and obedience to his Father.

The liturgy tells us that the faithful offer the sacrifice with the priest, for he says at the Offertory "My sacrifice and yours".[214] Pius XII suggests two ways in which the faithful can especially unite themselves with the sacrifice they offer: first, by having the same mind as Christ did in offering it; secondly, by making a sacrifice of their lives. He says that they actively offer the sacrifice with their High Priest.[215] St Margaret Mary Alacoque tells a newly ordained priest how she will be able to join him in offering Mass *through his mediation.*[216]

As every Mass is an act of Christ and the Church, no Mass is entirely private, even when said by a priest alone, for the whole Church is present through him and it is the offering of the Church. As de Lubac says, 'In each place the whole Church is present for the offering of the sacrifice.'[217] Colman O'Neill argues that far from private Masses being an exception from the rule, they are an extension of the same principle as makes the participation of a congregation desirable; private Masses are not contrary to the principle of communal celebrations.[218] Every Mass is an action of Christ, the High Priest, and an oblation of himself through his ordained minister. Pope Paul VI was quick to defend the value of 'private Masses' in *Mysterium Fidei* 32: as Christ is offered in every Mass that is celebrated, it is for the salvation of the world and can benefit those for whom it is offered, living and dead. A Mass said by a priest alone is still an act of Christ and the Church.

The value of private Masses was questioned by Fr Karl Rahner towards the end of the 1940s, in his article 'The Many Masses and the One Sacrifice'.[219] He objected that grace is not received

---

214. *Orate, fratres, ut meum ac vestrum sacrificium* in the original text of the Missal.
215. *Mediator Dei* 84-85.
216. *Letters* (TAN Books) p. 256.
217. *Splendour of the Church,* p. 106.
218. *New Approaches,* p. 26.
219. 'Die vielen Messen und das eine Opfer', *Zeitschrift für katholische Theologie* 71 (1949), pp. 257-317.

automatically but requires the co-operation of the faithful in sharing in the sacrifice. The application of the fruits of redemption to individuals depends on their disposition to receive them, Rahner said. O'Neill criticised him for making the effectiveness of the sacrifice depend on the devotion of the faithful taking part in it. Rahner also seemed to make it impossible for souls in Purgatory to benefit from Masses, since they are not present at them. But the dead in Purgatory are not separated from the love of Christ. The value of private Masses and of Masses offered for those not physically present depends on two things. First, the Mass cannot benefit others not present at it unless it is a sacrifice. Secondly, those not physically present are united with those present, for every Mass is the action of the whole Church, of which they too are members. Thus every Mass applies the redeeming power of the cross to the world.

The response of the Council of Trent to the Reformers who attacked the saying of private Masses and the system of stipends, was that the Mass is *more* than a banquet: it is also a propitiatory sacrifice for the living and dead. Nevertheless, Masses do not automatically benefit those for whom they are offered unless they have, or have died in, the right disposition of faith and repentance. St Thomas Aquinas' opinion was that Mass benefits others according to the measure of their devotion.[220]

To conclude this section. 'The Mass is a sacrifice because in it, in a sacramental and mystical manner, Christ's offering, immolation and priestly activity in heaven, become effectively present for us, while he simultaneously takes up the offering of the Church into his one sacrifice.'[221] This quotation also links this section with the previous one. 'Sacramental' means by signs, and 'mystical' means hidden.

---

220. ST 3a 79, 7 ad 2.
221. J O'Connor, *The Hidden Manna*, p. 240.

The Reformation and Trent

In his book, *Eucharistic Sacrifice and the Reformation,* Francis Clark refutes the charges of various Anglicans from the seventeenth century onwards, that the Church's doctrine of the sacrifice of the Mass in the Middle Ages was corrupted, and that by the end of the fifteenth century it was quite inconsistent and muddled. He shows that it cannot have become confused by the end of the Middle Ages, because it was then still substantially the same as it had been in the twelfth century, as we can see in the standard author Peter Lombard (c. 1100-1160), who largely based himself on the text of St John Chrysostom which we have quoted above. Clark notes that the Church's medieval doctrine of sacrifice preserved its consistency, because there was hardly any development of it for 250 years, from the time of Aquinas until the eve of the Reformation. Thus the reason, or motive, of the Reformers for attacking the sacrifice of the Mass cannot have been that this doctrine had become distorted by the year 1500 but must have been their own dislike of it.

Francis Clark found that the Church maintained a consistent doctrine of sacrifice throughout the Middle Ages. It cannot have degenerated or become muddled, since it was sound at the end of the thirteenth century and hardly changed in the next 250 years. It remained what it was in Peter Lombard, *Sentences* IV dist. 12:[222]

> We may briefly reply that what is offered and consecrated by the priest is called a sacrifice and an immolation, because it is a memorial and representation of the true sacrifice and holy immolation made upon the altar of the cross. Christ died once, upon the cross, and there he was immolated in his own person; and yet he is immolated sacramentally, because in the sacrament there is a recalling of what was once done.[223]

---

222. *Eucharistic Sacrifice and the Reformation,* p. 82
223. *Sentences* IV d. 12, 7 (PL 192, 866).

Peter Lombard recalls Chrysostom's principle that the sacrifice is the same, as there is one Christ everywhere. He anticipates St Thomas by over one hundred years in several phrases, for example, 'representation of the true sacrifice'. He answers two questions in his section on the Eucharist as a sacrifice:

Is the Eucharist properly a sacrifice?

Is Christ immolated once or many times?

His answer to the first question is that what is offered and consecrated by the priest is a sacrifice and oblation, because it is the memorial and representation of the true sacrifice and holy immolation that was carried out on the altar of the cross. Christ died once on the cross and was immolated in himself on it, but he is immolated daily in the sacrament, because the sacrament is the recalling of what was done once on the cross. Quoting the passage from Chrysostom on Hebrews (which he ascribed to St Ambrose), Lombard says that there is one victim (*hostia*), not many. There is one, not many, because Christ was only immolated once. The Eucharist is the same sacrifice, because one and the same thing is offered: one Christ is offered everywhere. As one and the same body is offered, so there is only one sacrifice. We now offer what was offered on the cross, but what we do is a recalling (*recordatio*) of the sacrifice.[224]

Much the same answers were given to these questions by later authors in the thirteenth, sixteenth and twentieth centuries, thus witnessing to a consistent tradition going back over nine hundred years.

Francis Clark summarises the Church's doctrine of sacrifice at the time of the Reformation in ten propositions.[225]

1. The Mass is a proper sacrifice.

2. Christ's passion is sufficient to atone for all sins of all time.

---

224. *Sentences IV* d. 12, 7.
225. Op. cit., pp. 93 f.

The offering of Mass does not imply that anything was lacking from Christ's passion.

3. Since Christ's priesthood is eternal, he established an order of priests, through which he could continue this sacrifice for all time.

4. The Mass is not a sacrifice in its own right but relatively, as it was instituted to represent the sacrifice of the cross.

5. It is not a mere commemoration, but Christ's body and blood are offered to the Father, because Christ is really present in the Eucharist.

6. The sacrifice on the altar is one with the sacrifice on the Cross. The victim and the one who offers it (through his priests) are the same.

7. But the Mass differs in the mode that the sacrifice is offered: the Mass is an unbloody, mystical sacrifice.

8. All the fruits of Redemption are made available through the Mass. The efficacy of the Mass flows from the Cross. It is a propitiatory sacrifice, since it is offered to take sins away.

9. The Mass does not justify the sinner without repentance.

10. The effects of the Mass extend to the living and the dead.

Clark's thesis is that a common, clear and coherent doctrine of the Eucharist and sacrifice existed around the year 1500.[226] He can show that there was a generally accepted body of doctrine at that time by the agreement of the nominalist Gabriel Biel with the Thomist Cardinal Cajetan (1469-1534).[227] Biel (d. 1495) is unexceptional on the sacrifice of the Mass and entirely in accord with Peter Lombard in his work, *Exposition of the Sacred Canon of the Mass*. He writes, for instance, that Christ is offered in the Mass 'not through a re-iterated death, but through the commemorative

---

226. Ibid., p. 95.
227. Ibid., p. 96.

representation of the death once suffered'.

Francis Clark shows that the idea that Christ is slain every time in the Mass was a figment of some Reformers, not part of Catholic belief. He disproves the charge made by Protestants, that the medievals equated the sacrifice with a daily slaying of Christ, and shows that the origin of this falsehood was a fallacy drawn by Zwingli in 1523. Zwingli misrepresented Catholic belief with the following argument:

> There is no sacrifice without immolation.
> The Mass is a sacrifice.
> Therefore Christ is immolated in the Mass.

It is a fantasy that the medievals thought that sacrifice implies a daily new immolation of Christ. This argument fails to take notice that the sacrifice is the same but offered in a different way in the Mass. As Clark shows, the theory that Christ is slain anew in every Mass was no part of Catholic theology in the late Middle Ages but a taunt of the Swiss Reformer.[228] The reply of Catholics was that Christ cannot be daily slain again, because he has risen to die no more (Rom 6:9). Although the Mass is a true sacrifice, Christ is not slain over and again, because, as Jan Eck said in 1528: 'As he was once offered on the cross really and corporeally, so now he is offered daily in an unbloody manner, in the mystery of this sacrifice.' Thus Eck refuted the Reformers' misconception of the Catholic doctrine by pointing to the *different way* in which the sacrifice is offered in the Mass.

Cajetan drew a distinction between the way Christ himself and the sacrifice are present in the Mass, in his pamphlet *Errors on a Booklet*, written against Zwingli in 1525. Christ's flesh and blood are signified *and* contained in the sacrament, but Christ's passion is only signified, not contained in it. 'Two things must be rightly understood: Christ himself is both signified and contained, while his death is indeed signified but not contained.' 'So Christ's body

---

228. Ibid., pp. 393-396.

and his Passion are present in different ways. The sacrifice was then offered in a material way, now it is offered in a spiritual manner.' Christ's one sacrifice is sufficient for all time; but many Masses are offered to apply its effects throughout the ages.

The body of doctrine that was current before the Reformation, as it is found in Biel and Cajetan, was subsequently codified at the 22nd session of the Council of Trent, in September 1562 under Pius IV, under the following points:

1. 'Christ left a sacrifice by which the bloody sacrifice which was accomplished on the cross could be represented.'[229]

2. By it the power of Christ's sacrifice is applied for the remission of sins.[230]

3. This sacrifice is truly propitiatory.[231]

The Council of Trent

Trent taught that the Mass has the same victim, offerer and effect as Calvary. Canon 3 reaffirms that the Mass is not just a sacrifice of praise and thanksgiving or a mere commemoration of the sacrifice on the cross but a true sacrifice. It benefits others besides those who take part in the Mass and receive communion. Thus Trent makes the following points against the Reformers:

1. It is not a mere memorial.

2. There is a different mode of offering the sacrifice in the Mass.

3. The Mass applies the one redemptive sacrifice to all mankind.

In answer to the accusation of the Reformers that the Mass was an ever new immolation of Christ and added to his once-and-for-all sacrifice, the Council of Trent replied that it was not just a banquet

---

229. Trent XXII c. 1 (DS 1740; ND 1546).
230. Loc. cit., (ND 1546).
231. Ibid., c. 2 (DS 1743; ND 1548).

but a propitiatory sacrifice for the living and dead, although it only benefits those with the necessary dispositions of faith and repentance.

Modern Theories of the Sacrifice

There have been three main theories about the sacrifice of the Mass since the Counter-Reformation:

1. The Mass is an *Immolation*: there is a destruction of the victim. At Mass this destruction occurs when the host and contents of the chalice are consumed by the priest in communion. This was the theory of St Robert Bellarmine (1542-1621). Cardinal Journet points out that Christ is not affected but only the sacramental signs are; the action of the Mass does not end in a destruction but in the sacramental presence of Christ.[232]

2. The Mass is an *Oblation*: it is the bringing of an offering. This was the theory of Père Maurice de Taille SJ, which will be explained below.

3. The Mass is a *Representation* of Christ's sacrifice on the Cross. This has been the view of many writers since the late 19th century, including the Benedictines Odo Casel and Anscar Vonier (a sacramental sacrifice). It was adopted by Pius XII in *Mediator Dei*, continued by Paul VI in *Mysterium Fidei*, and so has established itself as the leading theory today.

Maurice de Taille SJ (1872-1933) proposed that the Mass is the offering of the victim already immolated. We make a new offering of the once-for-all immolation. In de Taille's view, the Mass is a sacrifice because Christ virtually offered the sacrifice of his Passion at the Last Supper, when he made himself over to God. There was one and the same offering at the Last Supper and on the Cross. Since the Priest and Victim were the same, so de Taille

---

232. *La Messe*, p. 344.

argued, Calvary was but the immolation of the victim already offered at the Last Supper. The Mass is the same oblation as the Last Supper. 'It is one and the same thing to offer the body of Christ as having suffered and died in the Passion as to offer the Passion and death of the body; it is the same to offer the blood as shed as to offer its shedding; the same to offer Christ as victim of a past immolation as to offer the immolation itself.'[233] According to de Taille, Christ is offered in three ways:

1. At the Last Supper, to be immolated
2. On the Cross by being immolated
3. In the Mass, as immolated

De Taille, however, makes the Mass depend solely on the past sacrifice. He fails to notice that *Christ* is the Priest who principally offers the sacrifice of the Mass. Christ is not only passively offered in Mass but *actively* offers the sacrifice of himself in Mass every time. For de Taille, Christ's active sacrifice is only in the past. The Mass is a passive sacrifice as Christ's sacrifice of himself has been accepted by the Father through his Resurrection and Ascension. Thus the passive sacrifice of having been accepted remains forever. In this way de Taille links the Mass with the liturgy in heaven. De Taille noted that it was not Christ's death in itself but his loving obedience which made satisfaction for our sins. This view finds support in Hebrews 10:9 which says that Christ's sacrifice was one of his will, that is, of obedience. In this way, too, Christ's sacrifice is a *spiritual* one, for it does not consist in offering external victims (beasts) but one's own interior will. Francis Clark notes that two elements are required for a sacrifice: a victim and a ritual asking for acceptance.[234] Both these elements were present in the ritual oblation at the Last Supper.

For Vonier, the Mass is a sacramental sacrifice which represents the sacrifice on the Cross and thus renders it present, but it does not

---

233. *The Mystery of Faith*, pp. 23-24.
234. Op. cit., p. 254.

represent Christ offering himself but the death of Christ. Journet remarks that we do not have Christ dead but *living* in the Eucharist.[235]

In his encyclical *Mediator Dei* (1947), Pius XII favoured the view that the Mass is a sacrifice because it is a *sacramental representation* of the Cross. We have already encountered this view with Aquinas earlier in this chapter. Pius XII wrote that, as the transubstantiation of bread and wine brings about the real presence of Christ in the Eucharist, so the separate consecration of bread and wine make the one sacrifice present again. Christ's body and blood are really present but their separation is represented sacramentally at the consecration. At the Last Supper Christ offered his body and blood to the Father under the appearances of bread and wine.[236] At the altar the High Priest Christ does by an unbloody immolation, what he has already done of the Cross, offering himself to the eternal Father as a most acceptable victim.[237] The Mass is a 'commemorative showing forth' (*memorialis demonstratio*) of the sacrifice of the Cross.[238] The sacrifice on the Cross is re-presented, because there is the same Priest who offers the sacrifice in the Mass as on the Cross. Christ is represented by his priest, who acts *in persona Christi*.[239]

In line with Pius XII, Paul VI describes the Mass as a 'symbolic representation' of the sacrifice of the Cross. The unbloody immolation of Christ and the symbolic representation of the sacrifice of the Cross occur when Christ begins to be sacramentally present through the words of consecration.[240] This brings us back to the connection of the Sacrifice of the Mass with the Real Presence. Pope John Paul II speaks of 'the sacramental representation of Christ's sacrifice', but he connects it with the resurrection and thus keeps in view the *whole* Paschal mystery.[241]

---

235. *La Messe*, pp. 353 f.
236. *Mediator Dei* 71.
237. Ibid., 72.
238. Ibid., 74; ND 1566.
239. Ibid., 73.
240. *Mysterium Fidei* 34.
241. *Ecclesia de Eucharistia* 1, 15.

Sacrifice and Real Presence

The sacrifice of the Mass depends on the Real Presence of Christ's body and blood in the Eucharist. The Mass cannot be a sacrifice unless his body and blood are really present; otherwise we are just offering bread and wine to the Father after the consecration. Quoting from *Mysterium Fidei* 34, Colman O'Neill writes:

> There is, in other words, an intimate connection and interdependence between sacrifice and real presence. This is already indicated in 1 Corinthians, in the tenth chapter. The sacrifice and the sacrament, after all, belong to the same mystery; the one cannot be separated from the other. Christ is immolated sacramentally at the moment when, by the words of consecration, he begins to be sacramentally present as the spiritual food of the faithful under the appearances of bread and wine.[242]

The food given at communion is itself sacrificial; we partake in the sacrifice. This was St Paul's point in writing to the Corinthians: they were not to take part in sacrifices to idols when they partook of Christ's body and blood.

The inseparable connection between the Real Presence and the sacrifice is contained in the heart of the words of consecration, as we have already noted: "This is my body, which will be *given up* for you. This is the cup of my blood ... which will be *shed for many*." Their connection lies at the very centre of the mystery of the Eucharist. Thus we do not fully present the Mass to others when we only describe it as a 'meal' and omit to mention that it is also a sacrifice, which the Eucharist makes present again (re-presents).

Raymond Moloney rightly remarks that too often the Real Presence and the Sacrifice are considered apart when, in reality, they are integral. But where it is more common to hold that the

---

242. *New Approaches*, p. 55.

Eucharist's being a sacrifice depends on the Real Presence, Fr Moloney puts the sacrifice *before* the Real Presence. Rather than the Eucharist is a sacrifice because Christ is really present, he argues the other way round, from its being a sacrifice to the Real Presence. He thinks that the presence of Christ in the Eucharist is only intelligible in the context of his sacrificial action. Once one sees that it is a sacrifice, he says, one also sees that there has to be a change of bread and wine. Since the Eucharist is sacrificial, therefore Christ must be present, he argues. To support his view, Moloney invokes a principle of Aristotle's that action is the precondition of presence: that is, a thing is present where it is acting. For Aristotle, one body is present to another when it acts on it. Moloney then asks which action of Christ's grounds his presence in the Eucharist. The answer to this is: Christ's self-offering, which he enacted beforehand at the Last Supper. What makes the change of bread and wine meaningful for Moloney is the sacrifice, because what is given to us at communion is what Christ offers to his Father: namely, his body and blood.[243]

Moloney is supported by Karl Rahner, who may be Moloney's source for this view. Rahner denies that we offer Christ since he is present; rather Christ is present because the purpose of the Eucharist is sacrifice and food.[244] If Moloney's view is the right one, the sacrifice does not depend on the Real Presence, as I have argued above, but the Real Presence follows from the sacrifice. This is not the usual or natural way of looking at the Eucharist, and I ask whether it would be so fruitful in devotion to the Blessed Sacrament as focus on the Real Presence of Christ in the host has been since the thirteenth century. The Mass is surely a sacrifice, be-

---

243. *The Eucharist*, pp. 225-226.
244. *Christ in the Sacrament of the Lord's Supper*, *Theological Investigations IV* p. 309. Written in 1958, this essay compares the teaching of Trent with Luther's. In Rahner's view, transubstantiation does not say *how* the real presence comes about but affirms no more nor less than Christ's words do when taken simply.

cause what is offered after the consecration is the true body and blood of Christ. St Thomas inclines us towards the usual view that puts the Real Presence before the sacrifice, when he writes that the sacrament was primarily instituted for spiritual nourishment, not satisfaction.[245] The action that grounds Christ's presence in the Eucharist is rather the creative power of God's word changing bread and wine into his body and blood, which he gives up to his Father for us. Colman O'Neill is unequivocal that the Real Presence comes before the sacrifice, for he says that the primary aspect of the Eucharist is that it contains the body of Christ. He argues that communion, which is a gift from God, comes before sacrifice, which is the act of man.[246] Sacrifice and communion, however, are inseparable. Paul McPartlan links the two when he writes that, through the Eucharist, we are united with Christ and we are united with his Passion.[247] Like O'Neill, John Paul II also makes communion primary when he says that the sacrifice is directed to communion: in communion we receive him who offered himself for us on the cross.[248] Communion, however, not only gives us union with Christ but brings about the unity of Christ's body, the Church. It is to this second aspect of communion that we now turn.

---

245. ST 3a 79,5.
246. *Meeting Christ in the Sacraments*, pp. 189 f.
247. *The Eucharist*, p. 60.
248. *Ecclesia de Eucharistia* 1, 16.

Chapter 5

The Eucharist makes the Church

The Eucharist is not only the sacrament of Christ's real body and blood but is also the sign of the unity of his mystical body, the Church, which it brings about, for a sacrament is an *effective* sign: that is, it brings about what it signifies. Thus the Eucharist is, so to speak, a *double* sacrament: the sacrament of his real body and of the unity of his mystical body. As Pope John Paul II says, the Eucharist is 'the sacrament of ecclesial union'.[249] The two go together. This double aspect of the Eucharist is already stated for us by St Paul:

> The bread we break, is it not a participation in the body of Christ? Because there is one bread, we who are many are one body, for we all partake of one bread (1 Cor 10:16-17).

We should note here that St Paul uses the word 'body' in two ways: first, in a literal way of Christ's body when he says that the sacrament is a participation in the body of Christ; and secondly in a metaphorical sense, for many people are not literally one body. St Paul would not say that many are one body through partaking of Christ unless Christ now has his real body, because it was raised up to life again. Christians can only be said by analogy to be the body of Christ if he still has his body: they do not replace his body which died and was buried, nor are they his risen body. Indeed, they cannot be *incorporated* into his body unless he still has a body, into which they can be incorporated. Christ's body is not just the Church; his body is *risen*. Thus the second sense of 'body', by which many are one body, follows from, and depends

---

249. *Ecclesia de Eucharistia* 4, 43.

on, the first, that we participate in the real body of Christ in the Eucharist. This is the order of things in St Paul's words to the Corinthians, quoted above. Thus the Eucharist is the sacrament of the unity of the Church, *because* it is the sacrament of Christ's real body and blood.

The unity of the Church is compared by St Paul with the unity of a physical body:

> For as in one body we have many members ... so we, though many are one body in Christ, are individually members of one another (Rom 12:4-5).

We may note the last phrase, 'individually members of one another'. We are this through many people being one body in Christ, as a body consists of many members. It is like saying that all its members are members of one another, because they are all members of the same body. The foundation of the relation of Christ's real body to his mystical body, the Church, is the biblical concept of corporate personality, employed by St Paul in Romans 5:12-21: as all men die in Adam, so in Christ, the second Adam, all are made alive (Rom 5:18). All human beings derive physically from Adam, the first man, by nature; but they only become members of the last Adam by grace.

Similarly, St Paul also says:

> For just as the body is one and has many members, and all the members of the body, though many, are one body, so it is with Christ. For by one Spirit we were all baptised into one body (1 Cor 12:12-13).

We are incorporated into the body of Christ by baptism. It is the Spirit which brings together many members into the unity of this one body: in the Second Eucharistic Prayer, based on an ancient liturgy given by Hippolytus, we pray that 'all who share in the body and blood of Christ may be brought into unity by the Holy Spirit'. The Church is the mystical body of Christ, because all those who are incorporated into him are members of his body. As already mentioned in the previous chapter, the members of the Church are 'as though one mystical person' with Christ.[250]

The unity of Christ's mystical body, which the Eucharist brings about, presupposes that the Eucharist is the sacrament of his *real* body. Henri de Lubac said, 'ecclesial realism witnesses to Eucharistic realism'; the mystical body would not be united around a mere symbol.[251] In other words, the Eucharist is not the sacrament of the unity of the mystical body of Christ unless it is first the sacrament of his real body. The Church is not his body unless he still has his body, because it rose from the dead. Indeed, as we noted in chapter three, Aquinas says that Christ's body is present in the Eucharist, because the sacrament has a *relation* to his body in heaven. Thus the Eucharist does not just make his body, the Church, but presupposes that Christ has his real body, risen and now glorified in heaven.

In a long tradition, fully developed in St Augustine and going back to apostolic times, Aquinas sees the Eucharist as the sacrament of the unity of the Church in the signs of the sacrament, for bread is made out of many grains and wine from the juice pressed from many grapes. He writes: 'The Eucharist is called bread because it is the sacrament of the body of Christ, but the body of Christ is the Church, which rises (*consurgit*) into unity from many faithful people. Hence it is the sacrament of the unity of the Church. Because bread is made from many grains, so bread is the fitting sacramental appearance (*species*) of this sacrament.'[252] In the *Didache*, from around 100, it says that the unity of the mystical body is symbolised by the sacramental *species*, which are made out of many grains of wheat and many grapes.[253]

We speak, then, of the body of Christ in two ways: his body that is now glorified in heaven and is really present in the Eucharist,

---

250. Aquinas, ST 3a 48, 2 ad 1.
251. *Corpus Mysticum* pp. 289 f., quoted by C Journet, *La Messe*, p. 255.
252. *Super Ioannem* c. 6 lect. 5 (960).
253. *Didache* 9, 1-4, 10, 5-6.

and of his mystical body, the Church, which consists of many members united with the Head of the body, who is Christ. What is the relation between Christ's real and his mystical body? We should note that the Church is the mystical body *of Christ*; we do not speak of 'the mystical body of the Church'.

In answering this question, we should first keep in mind the exhortation of de Lubac:

> The Church, like the Eucharist, is a mystery of unity, the same mystery ... Both are the body of Christ, the same body. If we are faithful to Scripture, as Tradition interprets it, ... we must be careful not to make the smallest break between the Mystical Body and the Eucharist ... The two mysteries must be understood by one another.[254]

Just because they must be considered together does not mean, however, that they are identical. After all, the real body of Christ is present in the Eucharist; we do not say that his mystical body, the Church, is really present. What we receive in the Eucharist is not the Church but Christ himself. The Church is not *really* contained in the Eucharist, but Christ's body is. Rather the unity of the mystical body is the *effect* of the sacrament, which *is* the real body of Christ. As Paul McPartlan describes the view of de Lubac, Christians are not the eucharistic body of Christ but the Eucharistic body is Christ's real, personal body.[255] De Lubac himself was clear that the sacrament is the transformed elements, in other words, the body and blood of Christ. McPartlan seems rather to regret that de Lubac primarily saw the Eucharist as the transformed elements, for he wants the Eucharist to be the assembled *community*, that is, the Church.[256] But McPartlan shifts here between two uses of the word 'eucharist': as the body of Christ and as the liturgical action. In the first sense, for St Ignatius of

---

254. *The Splendour of the Church*, p. 110.
255. *The Eucharist Makes the Church*, p. 78.
256. Ibid., p. 73 (his italics).

Antioch, the Eucharist was also the flesh of Christ, as can be seen in our first quotation from him in chapter two.

De Lubac put forward the thesis in his book, *Corpus Mysticum*, that in the age of the Fathers the *corpus mysticum* (mystical body) was the body of Christ in the Eucharist. In his study of de Lubac, Paul McPartlan also holds that the *leitmotif* of the Fathers was that the Eucharist was the *mystical* body of Christ.[257] This was because the body was hidden, in *mysterio*, in the sacrament; so they called it the mystical body. But the real body of Christ for the Fathers, so de Lubac's thesis maintains, was the Church. 'But always the *corpus* par excellence, that which one thinks of in the first place, is the Church.'[258] After the eleventh century, however, what was the mystical body for the Fathers became the real body, and what was the real body became the mystical body. Here I would like to make two observations about de Lubac's thesis. First, it is not especially apparent from a representative sample of texts from the Fathers on the Eucharist, such as I have given in chapter two and may be found in any book on the Eucharist, that the real body was the Church; rather many of them were primarily concerned to show that the Eucharist was the flesh and blood of Christ. Secondly, de Lubac's thesis is supported by a wealth of quotations from *medieval* writers, many of them not well known, rather than by the main Fathers, with the exception of St Augustine. St Augustine is important on the Eucharist, and his doctrine of the whole Christ, Head and body together, is an important development, but, as already noted in chapter two, Augustine has comparatively little to say about what is the primary interest of most of the Fathers in the Eucharist, that it is the true body and blood of Christ.

McPartlan maintains that what was the mystical body for the Fathers became the real body, and vice-versa, in the eleventh century as a result of the controversy with Berengar of Tours, who admitted that Christ was mystically but not truly present

---

257. *Sacrament of Salvation*, p. 37.
258. *Corpus Mysticum* (Paris 1949) p. 34.

in the Eucharist.[259] Hence it became necessary for the Church to affirm that Christ is *really* present in the Eucharist. Consequently, as the real body in the Eucharist became Christ's own body, the term 'mystical' was then ascribed to his body, the Church. When the Church had to exclude Berengar's opinion that the Eucharist is not the true body but only a figure of it, the terms 'true' and 'mystical' were exchanged, so that from the 12th century onwards the body 'in a mystery', because hidden in this sacrament, became the true body. Another result of the controversy with Berengar, McPartlan notes, is that the emphasis moved from the Eucharist making the Church to how the Church makes the Eucharist, so that the Eucharist came to be seen on its own with the primary focus on the Real Presence. There is some truth in this but, as I have pointed out, the Eucharist as the sacrament of the unity of the mystical body of Christ presupposes the presence of his true body.

When we call the Church the 'mystical' body of Christ, we do not mean that she is merely a moral or invisible body, for the Church is a *visible* body. The union of her members is not purely invisible but also visible. Thus we have a visible sacrament to manifest the unity of the Church.

We gain some understanding of the relation of the real to the mystical body of Christ by recalling the threefold distinction of every sacrament in medieval theology. In every sacrament there is:

the sacrament alone (*sacramentum tantum*),

the sacrament and the reality (*sacramentum et res*),

the reality alone (*res tantum* or *res sacramenti*).

Our word reality comes from the Latin '*res*', a thing. The sacrament alone is the sign, which one sees: in the Eucharist, this is bread and wine. We have mentioned above how these can be signs of the unity of the Church, because they are made out of many grains and grapes. The sacrament and the reality are the

---

259. *Sacrament of Salvation*, p. 36.

supreme reality, in which one believes, says Journet.[260] Journet says that the reality alone is the effect which the sacramental body of Christ creates, which is to make his mystical body. And Aidan Nichols says that the *res sacramenti* means the purpose of the sacrament: this is union with Christ and with one another.[261] Nichols calls these the 'mystical' and 'ecclesial' dimensions of the sacrament.[262] John Paul II combines these two dimensions when he says, 'The Church is built up by sacramental communion with the Son of God, who was sacrificed for our sake.'[263] Colman O'Neill sees the order of the sacrament in the following way: the signified reality (*sacramentum et res*) is the body of Christ. The unity of the mystical body is the ultimate reality (*res tantum*), which is signified and effected by the physical body of Christ.[264] 'The mystical body is the fullness of the physical body.'[265] The Eucharist causes the unity of the mystical body, O'Neill says, because it causes charity. Thus the reality alone (*res tantum*) is the charity of the mystical body.[266] O'Neill also said that the purpose of the Eucharist is Christ's presence in the Church between the Ascension and the Second Coming.[267] For St Thomas Aquinas the *res sacramenti* was double: 'one is contained and signified, which is the integral Christ; the other is signified but not contained, and this is the mystical body of Christ, which exists in those who have been predestined, called and justified.'[268]

We talk of the body of Christ in three ways: the historic, sacramental and mystical body. His historic body is the body that was born of the Virgin, was crucified, rose again and is glorified in

260. *La Messe*, p. 252.
261. *The Holy Eucharist*, p. 78.
262. Ibid., p.76.
263. *Ecclesia de Eucharistia* 2, 21.
264. *Meeting Christ in the Sacraments*, p. 193.
265. Ibid., p. 188.
266. Ibid., pp. 193, 198.
267. *New Approaches*, p. 58.
268. *Super Ioannem* c. 6 lect 7 (972).

heaven. His sacramental body is the real body in the sacrament. His mystical body is the Church. The first is identical with the second. By sharing in the second we become part of the third; we eat his body to become his body. St Cyprian says that Christ gives his body to those who are members of his body: 'we call Christ our bread, because he is the food of those who are members of his body.'[269] Paschasius distinguishes between eating Christ's flesh (*caro*) and being in his body (*corpus*).[270]

Although there has been a tendency in recent decades to emphasise the communal aspect of the Eucharist at the expense of the primary reality of the sacrament, which is the true body and blood of Christ, the unity of the members of the Church is founded on their individual union with Christ. The reason why the participants are united with one another through receiving communion is that each one of them is united with one and the same person, Christ himself. Their union with one another is brought about by their individual union with Christ. St Thomas gives as the first purpose of the Eucharist: union with God in Christ and the grace of union with Christ:

> The effect of this sacrament ought firstly and mainly to be considered from what is contained in this sacrament, which is Christ.[271]

St Thomas' opinion seems also to be the present mind of the Church, as this is reflected in the universal *Catechism*. 'The principal fruit of receiving the Eucharist in Holy Communion is an intimate union with Christ Jesus.'[272] The *Catechism* then quotes John 6:56: 'Whoever eats my flesh and drinks my blood abides in me, and I in him'. The *Catechism* also says:

> The celebration of the Eucharistic sacrifice is wholly

---

269. *On the Lord's Prayer*, 18.
270. *De Corpore et Sanguine Domini* c. 7, PL 120, 1285.
271. ST 3a 79,1.
272. CCC 1391.

directed towards the intimate union of the faithful with Christ himself who has offered himself for us.[273]

Union with Christ, then, comes before the unity of the Church as the effect of this sacrament. Nevertheless, the two go together, for how can two people in union with Christ's body not be in union with one another? Perhaps the order of the two purposes of the Eucharist is put most succinctly by the *Catechism* thus: Christ 'makes us sharers of his body and blood to form a single body.'[274] For this reason the Eucharist is called *communion*. Although individual union with Christ comes first, we should not think of the Eucharist in the individualist way that was common in the past, since by communion we visibly express our union with the Church, through which we receive the Eucharist. The Eucharist cannot be separated from the Church. As Aidan Nichols says: we can only receive the Eucharist by being a part of Christ's body, the Church; we cannot share in the Eucharist when we stand outside the Church. You cannot have the purpose of the Eucharist outside the unity of the Church, because it is also the sacrament of unity as well as of the body and blood of Christ.[275] Pope John Paul II likewise emphasises that receiving the Eucharist presupposes communion with the Church and expresses it. He speaks of two unions, a visible and invisible one, as conditions for receiving the Eucharist: visible union with the Church, and invisible union with God through being in a state of grace.[276]

When we see the Eucharist as essentially a *double* sacrament, not only of the body and blood of Christ but also the sign of the unity of the Church, we can better understand the Church's rule about Intercommunion. Although this is thought by many to be a rather arbitrary decision of the Church, it follows from the nature of the sacrament itself. The Real Presence is not the only aspect

---

273. CCC 1382.
274. CCC 1331.
275. *The Holy Eucharist*, p. 79.
276. *Ecclesia de Eucharistia* 79.

to be considered; the Eucharist also expresses the unity of the Church. Anyone with this wider view of the Eucharist will see that to approach communion in any church is a visible sign that one is in union with the Church or ecclesial community whose communion he or she receives. One can only be in union with *one* body or church at a time. This is the meaning of the very word 'union'.

St Augustine noticed an interesting difference between ordinary food and the food of the Eucharist: ordinary food is changed into us when we eat it, but we become what we receive in the Eucharist. When we eat natural food it becomes part of us, but when we receive the Eucharist the reverse happens: we are changed into it. 'Nor will you change me into you, as the food of your flesh, but you will be changed into me' (spoken by Christ), Augustine writes in *Confessions* 7,10. Augustine applies this saying, however, in its original context not to the Eucharist but to the divine Word. Fifty years later St Leo the Great applied it straight to the Eucharist: 'Participation in the body and blood of Christ does nothing other than that we pass over into what we receive.'[277] As already noted, St Augustine does not have much to say about the Real Presence but goes straight from the elements of the sacrament to its effect, the unity of the Church. This is because he is interested in the *whole* Christ, who is Head and members together. 'Head and members are one Christ', he says.[278] We are members of what we receive, which is the Body of Christ. We are one body made up of many members as bread is made of many grains. Augustine exhorts Christians to become what they receive in the Eucharist:

"The Body of Christ", you are told and you answer "Amen".
Be members then of the Body of Christ, so that your "Amen"
may be true. Why is this mystery accomplished with

---

277. *Sermo de Passione* 12, 7.
278. *Enarratio in Ps. 54*, 3.

bread? We shall say nothing of our own about it; rather let us hear the Apostle, who speaking of the sacrament says: "We being many are one body, one bread." Understand and rejoice. Unity, devotion, charity! One bread: and what is this one bread? One body made up of many ... Be then what you see and receive what you are.[279]

We notice how much Augustine draws from just reflecting on the elements used in the Eucharist. 'Be what you see', he says – this is, one bread or one body. 'Receive what you are' – the Body of Christ. We become Christ's body, the Church, by feeding on his body. We are incorporated into his body by eating his body.

St Augustine concludes that when we receive the Eucharist, 'Not only do we become Christians; we become Christ ... If he is the Head and we the members, then together he and we are the whole man.'[280] As de Lubac says, 'Head and members make one single body: Bridegroom and Bride are one flesh. There are not two Christs, one personal, the other "mystical".'[281] The source of our unity in the mystical body of Christ is the Incarnation, which in Tradition has been seen as a marriage of divine with human nature. Writing about the Annunciation, St Thomas says 'There is a certain spiritual marriage between the Son of God and human nature.'[282] In a marriage two become one flesh or one body; it is a union, as there is a union of divine and human nature in Christ. The marriage of Christ and the Church, which began with the marriage of human and divine nature in the womb of Mary, is also symbolised by the marriage feast of Cana.[283]

St Augustine describes the Eucharist as 'the sacrament of devotion, the sign of unity, the bond of charity.'[284] The Eucharist

---

279. *Sermon 272.*
280. *Tract on John 21,8.*
281. *Splendour of the Church*, p. 112.
282. ST 3a 30, 1.
283. O'Connor, *The Hidden Manna*, p. 348.
284. *Tract on John 26,13.*

is a sign of unity, because it is the sacrament of charity. It is the sacrament of charity, because it represents the Passion of Christ, in which above all he showed his immense love by laying down his life for us. It is also the sacrament of charity, because he instituted the Eucharist at the Last Supper, when Christ gave the disciples the New Commandment, to love one another as he loved them. As the Eucharist is the sacrament of love, so it is also that of unity. Thus the Eucharist is inseparable from the Church, which includes the communion of saints. The Church on earth, the souls in Purgatory and the saints in heaven are all one Church. Since they are all united in one body, those on earth can help those in Purgatory by offering the sacrifice of this one body for them; and we can be helped by the prayers of the saints in heaven. By sharing in holy things (the sacraments) we also have communion with the saints. It is the same phrase in Latin for communion of holy things and communion of saints, *communio sanctorum*. This phrase in the Creed may mean either.

The Eucharist makes the Church

The Eucharist, as we have already noted, is both the sign and the cause of the unity of the mystical body of Christ. It brings about what it expresses and is the sign of it. The unity of the faithful in the one body of the Church is brought about and expressed by the Eucharist.

> As often as the sacrifice of the Cross, by which "Christ our Passover is Sacrificed" (1 Cor 5:7), is celebrated on the altar, the work of our redemption is carried out. Likewise, in the sacrament of the eucharistic bread, the unity of believers, who form one body in Christ, is both expressed and brought about.[285]

St Augustine says that the Eucharist is the sacrament 'by which

---

285. LG 1,3.

the Church is now united.'[286] The Church is made by her members being united ever more fully and closely with Christ's body.

> The unity of the Mystical Body: the Eucharist makes the Church. Those who receive the Eucharist are united more closely with Christ. Through it Christ unites them to all the faithful in one body – the Church. Communion renews, strengthens and deepens this incorporation into the Church, already achieved by baptism. In baptism we have been called to form but one body. The Eucharist fulfils this call.[287]

The writer of this part of the *Catechism* was no doubt thinking of de Lubac's phrase, 'The Eucharist makes the Church.' The French word used by de Lubac for 'makes' here is *'réalise'*: literally, the Eucharist realises the Church.[288]

> The Eucharist is the effective sign of the spiritual sacrifice offered to God by the whole Christ; for the sacrifice of Christians is such that all, in the fullness of their numbers, are one single body in Christ. The Church thus really makes herself by the celebration of this mystery.[289]

We may note two things here. Not for the first time, the making of the Church is linked with the sacrifice of the Eucharist. Just as the old covenant with Israel was sealed with the sprinkling of blood by Moses (Ex 24:8), so the new and everlasting covenant was made with the new Israel when Christ represented his sacrifice on Calvary at the Last Supper by offering the disciples his body and blood as food.[290] The Church was originally made in the sacrifice of the Cross, when blood and water flowed from the pierced side of Christ (Jn 19:34). The blood and water that flowed from Christ's

---

286. *Contra Faustum* 12, 20.
287. CCC 1396.
288. *Splendour of the Church*, p. 92.
289. Ibid., p. 108.
290. *Ecclesia de Eucharistia* 2, 21.

side on the cross were taken by the Fathers of the Church to symbolise the sacraments of Baptism and the Eucharist, which build the Church.[291] Paul McPartlan makes a nice connection between the water that came from Christ's side on the cross and the water that flows from the heavenly city.[292] Pope John Paul II touches on the same theme when he writes, 'The institution of the Eucharist sacramentally anticipated the events' of the paschal mystery, out of which the Church was born.[293]

Secondly, we notice how this thought of de Lubac influenced the Second Vatican Council, for instance, in the quotation from *Lumen Gentium* above. The Church makes herself by celebrating the sacrament of Christ's body. The Church is the body of Christ, because it is made by the sacrament of his true body, which unites her members with Christ. Paul McPartlan writes that, by receiving 'the bread which has become his body, we are united in his Body which is the Church.'[294]

The Eucharist makes the Church, because those who share in the body and blood of Christ are also united one with another in one body, so that they form the Church. At the same time, the Church makes the Eucharist, for there is no Eucharist without the Church. Without the Church, there is neither any priest to consecrate bread and wine, nor anyone to gather to celebrate Mass and offer the sacrifice with the priest. The Church makes the Eucharist, de Lubac says, because the Eucharist makes the Church.[295] They make each other. This thought has been included by John Paul II in his encyclical on the Eucharist: 'The Eucharist builds the Church and the Church makes the Eucharist.'[296] But what enables us to be in the unity of the Church is our union with Christ: 'Our

---

291. See, for example, Augustine, *The City of God*, XXII, 17.
292. *Sacrament of Salvation*, p. 10.
293. *Ecclesia de Eucharistia* 3.
294. *The Eucharist* (CTS) p. 18.
295. Op. cit., p.106.
296. *Ecclesia de Eucharistia* 3, 26.

union with Christ, which is a gift of a grace for each of us, makes it possible for us in him, to share in the unity of his body which is the Church.'[297]

According to Paul McPartlan, the Church which the Eucharist makes is the Church in heaven. The Eucharist does not so much signify the unity of the present Church as make the *future* Church in heaven, the Church as she *will* be when she is complete. 'Thus when de Lubac says the Eucharist makes the Church, it is the heavenly Church, within the eucharistic veil that he intends.'[298] In order to support his view, McPartlan appeals to a text in Hebrews:

> But you have come to Mount Sion and the city of the living God, the heavenly Jerusalem, and to innumerable angels in festal gathering, and the assembly of the first-born ... and to Jesus, the Mediator of the new covenant, and to the sprinkled blood that pleads more powerfully than the blood of Abel (Heb 12:22-24).

The festal gathering and the assembly (*ekklesia*), McPartlan says, is the liturgy, in other words, the Eucharist. What Christians come to in the Eucharist is the heavenly Jerusalem, that is, the Church in heaven.[299] The setting is the Eucharist, the gathering is the Church in heaven. For confirmation of his interpretation, McPartlan quotes an early text about the Eucharist in the *Didache:*

> As this broken bread, once dispersed over the hills, was brought together and became one loaf, so may the Church be brought together from the ends of the Earth into thy kingdom.[300]

There seems to be no reason, however, why this text does not mean the present Church on Earth that will be gathered into the

---

297. Ibid., 2, 23.
298. *The Eucharist Makes the Church*, p. 85.
299. *Sacrament of Salvation*, p. 4.
300. *Didache* 9.

Kingdom. This is surely an equally natural way of reading it.

When we say that the Eucharist is the sacrament of the mystical body of Christ, it seems more natural to think of the Church as she is *now,* for we who are united by sharing in the sacrament are part of the present Church. McPartlan himself notices that his view seems rather unexpected, for he comments that logic can sometimes be a barrier to understanding the Gospel, as though he felt that this view might appear to be against logic. Logic, however, can never be a barrier to understanding the Gospel because, though faith is above reason, it is not against reason. Indeed, logic takes its name from the Word (*Logos*). When an author requires us to accept something contrary to reason, we may well suspect whether his view is right. The thesis of McPartlan in his book, *Sacrament of Salvation,* is that the Eucharist signifies the Church when she will be perfect in the future. One argument against this view is that a sacrament cannot be the sign of something future that is not yet present, for it is not yet a reality. The sacraments are of *present* grace, although they may also look forward to the future fulfilment of a present reality in heaven. We may note that Aquinas counts the unity of the Church to be the *present* meaning, or signification, of the Eucharist.[301]

For McPartlan, the real body of Christ is the Church, the heavenly community. We notice that he reserves 'Body' with a capital 'B' for Christ's body, the Church, and uses 'body' with a lower-case 'b' when referring to Christ's real body and blood. There can be little doubt that the Church uses the word 'real' for Christ's body and blood really present in the Eucharist. But McPartlan admits that the future reality is 'mysteriously' present.[302] 'The Church is present from the future,' he says, just as Christ is present in the Church and in the Eucharist from the past.[303] He fails to note, however, that the past and future are not symmetrical, for some-

---

301. ST 3a 73, 4.
302. *Sacrament of Salvation,* p. 66.
303. *The Eucharist Makes the Church,* p. 89.

thing past has been a reality, whereas what is still future has not yet existed. Surely, the Church which the Eucharist signifies is what she now is on earth, also united with the Church of angels and saints in heaven. The Church in heaven is made out of the Church on earth. We participate in the heavenly Church 'in anticipation', McPartlan says,[304] but this participation is also now in the present.

The Church whose unity the Eucharist signifies is the present Church, which is one with the Church in heaven. If the Church that the Eucharist makes is still in the future, she is not already one with the mystical body of Christ that exists now. Thus the Church we come into contact with in the liturgy of the Eucharist is the present Church that is one with the Church in heaven even now. But the liturgy performed on earth participates in the liturgy that goes on in heaven. This will be the topic of our next chapter.

---

304. Ibid., p. 88.

Chapter 6

The Heavenly Liturgy

The Eucharist has a past, present and future dimension. We have considered its past reference to the sacrifice of the Cross, and its present dimension of the Real Presence and the unity of the Church. We now turn to its future dimension as it looks forward to the heavenly banquet. This banquet is already spoken about in Isaiah 25:6-8, as a feast on the Holy Mountain for all the peoples.

When we join our hymn of praise and thanksgiving in the Preface of the Mass to the song of the angels and saints in heaven, the Thrice Holy, we participate in the liturgy that goes on without ceasing in heaven before the throne of the Lamb.

> In the earthly liturgy we share in a foretaste of that heavenly liturgy which is celebrated in the Holy City of Jerusalem, towards which we journey as pilgrims, where Christ is sitting at the right hand of God, Minister of the sanctuary and true tabernacle. With all the warriors of the heavenly army we sing a hymn of glory to the Lord; venerating the memory of the saints, we hope for some part and fellowship with them; we eagerly await the Saviour, our Lord Jesus Christ, until he, our life, shall appear and we too will appear with him in glory.[305]

The future aspect of the Eucharist, that of recalling Christ's death *until he comes again*, reminds us that the Eucharist will only find its fulfilment in heaven.

> At the Last Supper the Lord himself directed the disciples' attention towards the fulfilment of the Passover in

---

305. CCC 1090.

the kingdom of God: "I tell you I shall not drink again of the fruit of the vine until that day when I drink it new with you in my Father's kingdom" (Mt 26:29). Whenever the Church celebrates the Eucharist she remembers this promise and turns her gaze "to him who is to come". In her prayer she calls for his coming: Maranatha! "Come, Lord Jesus".[306]

Pope John Paul II also says that it is by offering the sacrifice of the Mass that we participate in the heavenly liturgy: 'in celebrating the sacrifice of the Lamb, we are united to the heavenly "liturgy" and become part of that great multitude which cries out: "Salvation belongs to our God who sits upon the throne, and to the Lamb" (Rev 7:10).'[307] It is because we have communion with the saints through participating in the heavenly liturgy that we venerate Mary, the Mother of God, and the saints and ask for their intercession in the Mass. What is this heavenly liturgy, in which the Eucharist will find its fulfilment? It is the unceasing Adoration of the Lamb, 'as though slain', described in the Apocalypse. What the angels and saints celebrate in heaven is the victory of the Cross: 'Worthy is the Lamb who was slain, to receive power and wealth and wisdom and might and honour and glory and blessing' (Rev 5:12). The Lamb who is adored by the heavenly company is the Lamb of sacrifice, 'as though slain'. The same sacrifice as is re-presented in the Eucharist is perpetuated in heaven for all eternity. McPartlan points out that we can only truly speak of the victory of the Cross in the light of the Resurrection.[308] The Lamb that was slain is now risen and living for ever.

Descriptions of this liturgy are given in the Apocalypse.

> After this I looked, and behold a great multitude ... standing before the throne of the Lamb ... and crying out

---

306. CCC 1043; 1 Cor 16:22.
307. *Ecclesia de Eucharistia* 1, 19.
308. *Sacrament of Salvation*, p. 24.

with a loud voice, "Salvation belongs to our God who sits upon the throne, and to the Lamb" (Rev 7:9-10).

Then I looked, and lo, on Mount Sion stood the Lamb ... And I heard a voice from heaven ... like the sound of harpers playing on their harps, and they sing a new song (Rev 14:1-3).

McPartlan sees the assembly in heaven as the model of the gathering of the hierarchy and faithful at the Eucharist on earth. The faithful are gathered around the priest at Mass as the multitude in heaven is gathered around the throne of the Lamb, who is our great High Priest.[309]

In the Eucharist, we give thanks for the same triumph of the Lamb who has redeemed a great multitude by his blood,[310] as is celebrated in heaven by the angels and saints. As we look back to Christ's Passion and sacrifice at Mass we also look forward to sharing in its celebration in heaven. The Second Vatican Council's document on the liturgy says that, in the Mass, we both perpetuate the sacrifice of the cross and have a foretaste of the heavenly liturgy.[311] Paul McPartlan observes that these two aspects, which are the past and future ones, go together. [312] He says that the Mass perpetuates the sacrifice by being a foretaste of the heavenly liturgy.[313] The Mass, however, is not a sacrifice because it participates in the heavenly liturgy but because Christ, through the hands of his minister, offers the sacrifice of the Mass to his Father. It is the Holy Spirit who enables us to participate in the heavenly liturgy.

It is in this eternal liturgy that the Spirit and the Church enable us to participate whenever we celebrate the mystery of salvation in the sacraments.[314]

---

309. Ibid., p.11.
310. Rev 7:14.
311. SC 47 and 8.
312. *The Eucharist* (CTS) p. 28.
313. Ibid., p. 31.
314. CCC 1139.

At Mass we do in signs what is done for ever in heaven.

The heavenly liturgy perpetuates the sacrifice once offered on the cross, because our High Priest has entered into the Holy of Holies by his Ascension, taking with him his human nature that was offered on the Cross, in order to plead for us with it at the right hand of his Father.[315] As the high priests used to enter the Holy of Holies through the veil of the Temple, so Christ has opened up for us a new and living way through the curtain of his flesh. By offering up his body in sacrifice, he has opened up for us 'a new and living way' into the true sanctuary in heaven.[316] Our way into it is through the humanity of Christ (the veil of his flesh).

The Mass is related to the heavenly liturgy, because it represents the sacrifice which is perpetuated through the Adoration of the Lamb. The liturgy in heaven itself prolongs the sacrifice of the Cross. Christ our High Priest, who offered himself up as a victim on the Cross, is now seated at the right hand of the Father in heaven.[317] There he intercedes for us with his wounded humanity, which was offered in sacrifice and accepted by the Father in his Resurrection and Ascension. The Mass, however, is *directly* related to the Cross: it is not a sacrifice *via* the heaven liturgy. 'It was expressly for the perpetual re-presentation of that death that Our Lord instituted the Holy Sacrifice on the night that he was betrayed.'[318] The Mass represents the sacrifice which was taken up to heaven at the Ascension and is now perpetuated there for ever.[319] Francis Clark observes that when we see the Mass as a participation in the heavenly liturgy, this helps to defend the doctrine of the sacrifice of the Mass, precisely because the Mass represents that sacrifice which is perpetuated forever in the

---

315. Heb 9:12.
316. Heb 10:20.
317. Heb 8:1.
318. F Clark, *Eucharistic Sacrifice and the Reformation*, p. 293.
319. Ibid., p. 285.

adoration of the Lamb 'as though slain.' Francis Clark, however, warns us against being unduly influenced by the great emphasis on the heavenly liturgy which only became a part of Byzantine theology at a comparatively late stage, after AD 1000.[320] It is wrong to see the Passion just as a preliminary of the intercession of our High Priest in heaven for ever; rather this second only prolongs the first. It is by the first that Christ atoned for sins.

The Adoration of the Lamb that was sacrificed is also the Wedding Feast of the Lamb. The liturgy that perpetuates the sacrifice of the Lamb is also the heavenly banquet. At the wedding-feast of the Lamb and his bride, the Church, all those called to it praise and adore the Lamb once slain in the unceasing liturgy of heaven. The four-and-twenty elders and the four living creatures (symbols of the evangelists) fall down and worship God on his throne, saying "Amen" ('It is true'), and a great multitude cries 'Let us rejoice, for the marriage of the Lamb has come, and his bride has made herself ready.'[321] (In the Old Testament, marriage is a common image of the union of God and his chosen people.) The Eucharist is the foretaste on earth of the heavenly banquet that is also the marriage-feast of the Lamb and his bride, the Church. This heavenly banquet is meant in the Parable of the Wedding Feast that the King gives for his Son, Christ.[322] The parable is about the Eucharist on earth and its fulfilment in the kingdom of God at the same time. Those gathered from the bye-ways and country roads are also the many who will come from East and West to sit at table with Abraham, Isaac and Jacob in the Kingdom.[323] Both those called to the Eucharist on earth and those sitting at the banquet in heaven with the Patriarchs, are united in the one Church which spans heaven and earth across all time.

---

320. Ibid., p. 292.
321. Rev 19:7.
322. Mt 22:1-14.
323. Mt 8:11; Luke 13:28 with a different context.

Chapter 7

The Eucharist in Ecumenical Dialogue

In an address in Poland, 8 June 1987, Pope John Paul II declared that the goal of all ecumenical dialogue is that all Christians come to share in celebrating the same Eucharist. *Unitatis Redintegratio* 2 stated that 'Christ instituted the wonderful sacrament of the Eucharist, by which the unity of the Church is both signified and brought about.' Discussion about the Eucharist has thus a central part in, and holds the key to, the uniting of Christians under one Shepherd with the same sacraments. The Eucharist is indeed the sacrament of unity. At the Reformation, the doctrine of the Eucharist was one of the two major areas of dispute between Catholics and Reformers (the other was Justification). In this chapter, we shall see to what extent Anglicans and the World Council of Churches think alike again with the Catholic Church about the Eucharist. We shall also give some account of the Orthodox perspective on the Eucharist, where the difference is more one of approach than of any error or deficiency of belief. For the Orthodox draw from the Fathers of the Eastern Church who are part of the one Tradition of the Church. We should bear in mind that the Catholic Church has a different relationship to the Orthodox churches and the Reformed, or Protestant, communities. The Second Vatican Council, in its decree on ecumenism, said that the Eastern churches have valid sacraments but are 'not in full communion with the Catholic Church.'[324] But 'the communities of the Reformation' are separated from the Catholic Church; they are not called 'churches' but 'ecclesial communities'.[325]

---

324. *Unitatis Redintegratio* 15.
325. Ibid., 22.

ARCIC

In 1971 the Anglican-Roman Catholic International Commission produced an Agreed Statement on the Eucharist. This was published in the *Final Report* on Authority, Eucharist and Ministry ten years later, in 1981, together with some 'Elucidations' in the light of discussion of the Agreed Statement in the intervening years. One of the main difficulties in reaching agreement is not so much between Anglicans and Catholics but within the Anglican Communion itself. This became clear in the Elucidations of 1979, which revealed that not everyone within the bodies represented on the Commission was happy with what their representative had approved in the Agreed Statement. Thus it is difficult to be sure that one has secured agreement and unity of view with all the members of other communions even when they have officially signed an 'agreed' statement.

The Agreed Statement of 1971 makes the following admissions about the Real Presence:

Bread and wine 'become his body and blood' (6).

'The elements are not mere signs; Christ's body and blood become really present and are really given' (9).

'Bread and wine become the body and blood of Christ by the action of the Holy Spirit, so that in communion we eat the flesh of Christ and drink his blood' (10).

Although these passages affirm the real presence, and even that Christ's body and blood are received in communion, the strongest word they use for how this comes about is 'become'; at no point do they admit that bread and wine are *changed*. Mention of 'transubstantiation' was relegated to a footnote of paragraph 6.

There is no mention of reservation of the Blessed Sacrament, although it is found in some Anglican parish churches now. Nor is the Eucharist said to be a sacrifice for the forgiveness of the sins of the living and dead. It only says that we must connect the sacrifice with Christ's once-and-for-all sacrifice, which is an important principle. A significant step towards reaching a common understanding about the sacrifice was achieved by introducing the biblical term of '*anamnesis*', which means to recall an event in a way that also makes it present again. The sacrifice of the Cross is only made present again, or re-presented, however, when Christ's body and blood are really present, as was pointed out in chapter four.

The Elucidations of 1979 contained the Commission's responses to criticisms of the Agreed Statement. These revealed that it was not accepted by many represented on the Commission. For some, even the word 'became' was too strong for describing what happens to bread and wine in the Eucharist. Others thought that the real transformation is not of bread and wine in the sacrament itself but of the persons who receive it into the likeness of Christ. This is, so to speak, the interior effect of the sacrament without its objective reality. This view does not explicitly admit that the Eucharist really *is* the body and blood of Christ. In *A Critique of Eucharistic Agreement*, John Lawrence pointed out that for many Anglicans to receive Christ's body and blood means little more than to share in his life.[326]

In his summary of the main achievements of ARCIC I on the Eucharist, Aidan Nichols lists the following two points of agreement:

1. The Eucharist is the *effective* memorial of Christ's sacrifice. It is the sacramental expression of Christ's sacrifice.

2. There is a real but spiritual presence of Christ in the Eucharist. (Spiritual means not natural, in other words, sacramental.)

Nichols also observes that ARCIC I looked back to biblical and Patristic sources but overlooked the Middle Ages and the contemporary practice of the Catholic Church.[327]

---

326. *A Critique*, p. 29.
327. *The Holy Eucharist*, p. 132.

When the Congregation for the Doctrine of the Faith finally produced its own judgement of the *Final Report* a further ten years on, it found it deficient in the following areas:

1. Mention of the propitiatory value of the sacrifice had been omitted.

2. It is not clear that the Church, through the ministry of Christ's priests, offers the sacrifice of Christ in him and with him.

3. Some passages do not adequately indicate what the Church means by transubstantiation, namely that bread and wine do not remain.

4. Following from this, there is divergence about adoration of the Sacrament. The Congregation said that any adequate agreed statement would have to include veneration of the reserved Sacrament. (Paul VI devotes a special section to this in *Mysterium Fidei* 67-70).

The net result was that a breakthrough was achieved in understanding the Eucharist as a sacrifice by returning to the biblical notion of *anamnesis*. But to do justice to the Catholic belief in the Real Presence, it is also necessary to insist on the total *change* of bread and wine into Christ's body and blood, so that nothing of bread and wine remains after the consecration except their appearances.

At the time the Agreed Statement was published, many Catholics in this country thought that this was now what the Catholic Church believed and taught about the Eucharist. This was a misunderstanding. An agreed statement can only represent what is common to the belief of all parties; it is not a complete teaching. The Agreed Statement did not signal any alteration or reduction of the Church's doctrine, but only let us know how much of this was now officially accepted by the Anglican communion.

Lima

At the same time as the *Final Report* of ARCIC I came out, the World Council of Churches produced its own agreed statement on *Baptism, Eucharist and Ministry,* often referred to as the 'Lima' document after the city where the discussions were held. It was published in Geneva in 1982. This was not an agreed statement between Catholics and the Reformation communions but among the members of the World Council of Churches themselves. It does, however, invite comparison with Catholic doctrine as a measure of unity so far existing.

Lima describes the Eucharist variously as a 'meal' or 'sacramental meal', which by sacramental signs communicates to us God's love in Jesus Christ.[328] It is the sacrament of the gift of God, that is, of eternal salvation. 'In the eating and drinking of the bread and wine', Christ grants communion with himself.[329] Later it speaks more biblically of 'sharing in one bread and one cup': 'Sharing in one bread and one cup is communion with the Body of Christ, which is the Church.'[330] 'The Eucharist meal' is 'the sacrament of the body and blood of Christ, the sacrament of his real presence.'[331] *Lima* nominally, or verbally, affirms the Real Presence, but does not say how it comes about or that the sacrament *is* the Body and Blood of Christ. It only admits that Christ's words, spoken at the consecration, are true: 'What Christ declared (This is my body ... This is the cup of my blood) is true, and this truth is fulfilled every time the Eucharist is celebrated.'[332]

There seems here to be a progression of statements towards a more fully Catholic point of view. The latter phrases about real presence and truth are hardly consistent with the first, which speak about sharing in bread and wine and, quite vaguely, of receiving the gift of God's love or salvation. Nor does *Lima* say what it means by the sacramental signs: are these bread and wine, which would then still remain after the consecration, or the *appearances* of bread and wine?

---

328. *Eucharist* I 1.
329. Ibid., II 2.
330. Ibid., II D 19.
331. Ibid., II B 13.
332. Ibid., II B 13.

This doubt remains even though it says that, in virtue of the word of Christ and the power of the Holy Spirit, 'bread and wine become sacramental signs of Christ's body and blood.'[333] This phrase rather suggests that bread and wine remain. Nowhere does *Lima* affirm that the Eucharist is the Body and Blood of Christ; rather it only gives us communion with his Body, the Church.[334] The *Lima* document says little that is definite about sacrifice, being weaker in this area than the Final Report of ARCIC I, except that it declares 'The Eucharist is the sacrament of the unique sacrifice of Christ.'[335] It also calls the Eucharist a 'representation'. Mention of the power of the Holy Spirit brings us to the distinctive contribution that the Orthodox Church has to make to our understanding of the mystery of the Eucharist.

The Orthodox Perspective

In this country we easily forget that the main ecumenical dialogue of the Church as a whole is not with Anglicans but with the Orthodox, reunion with whom Pope John Paul II made one of the major objectives of his pontificate. When we come to the Orthodox Church, it is not a question of heresy but of different approaches, for the Orthodox retain valid sacraments. In 1982, a joint commission of the Orthodox and Catholic Church produced their first agreed statement, with the title '*The Mystery of the Church and of the Eucharist in the Light of the Mystery of the Trinity*'.[336] I shall just call it '*Mystery*' for short. It serves well to increase our knowledge of the overall Tradition about the Eucharist, where the West has forgotten perspectives retained by the East.

On the role of the Holy Spirit in effecting the sacrament, the joint Orthodox and Roman Catholic commission says, 'The Spirit transforms the sacred gifts into the Body and Blood of Christ'.

333. Ibid., II B 15.
334. Ibid., II D 19.
335. *Lima* II B8, quoted by P McPartlan, *The Eucharist*, p. 59.
336. Reprinted in P McPartlan, *One in 2000?*, pp. 53-69.

The Orthodox see the entire celebration of the Eucharist as an invocation (*epiclesis*) of the Holy Spirit on the gifts and the assembly. Thus the Holy Spirit both changes the gifts and brings about the unity of the Church, which the Eucharist signifies. By making present 'the event of the mystery', which is what Christ did once-for-all to redeem us, the Spirit accomplishes the mystery in us. Thus the Eucharist is the centre of sacramental life, because our relation to the Spirit is made more evident by it. The Son communicates the Spirit to us particularly in the Eucharist. The document notes that the Holy Spirit had not yet been poured out when Christ instituted the Eucharist at the Last Supper. The 'energies' of the Holy Spirit are now at work in the Church. The Eucharist is the sacrament of the divinising love of the Father through the Son in the Holy Spirit.[337] The Holy Spirit is 'the agent of unity in plurality': that is, he makes many be one. The same thought can be found in the Western tradition too, in Aquinas who says: 'For the unity of the Church is made by the Holy Spirit.'[338]

Thus the Spirit brings it about that the Eucharist makes the Church. 'The Holy Spirit reveals the Church as the Body of Christ, which he constitutes and makes grow. When the Church celebrates the Eucharist, she realises what she is, the Body of Christ.'[339] The Church is fully herself when she is at the *synaxis* (gathering) of the Eucharist. 'The Church celebrates the Eucharist as the expression here and now of the heavenly liturgy; but, on the other hand, the Eucharist builds up the Church in the sense that through it the Spirit of the risen Christ fashions the Church into the Body of Christ.'[340] So both the Holy Spirit and the Eucharist make the Church, or the Holy Spirit does so through the Eucharist.

The Church is herself the sacrament of the Trinitarian *koinonia*

---

337. *One in 2000?*, p. 44
338. *Super Ioannem* c. 6 lect. 7 (972).
339. *One in 2000?*, p. 39.
340. Ibid., p. 39.

(communion), that is, of the dwelling of God with men.[341] The mystery of the unity of many persons in love constitutes the newness of Trinitarian *koinonia*, communicated to men and women in the Church through the Eucharist. This koinonia is first of all the indwelling of the Three Persons of the Trinity, each in the other, which is then reproduced in us. More will be said about the indwelling of the Trinity as an effect of the Eucharist in chapter eight. As the Holy Spirit is the agent of unity, he brings together the Church, who reflects in herself the koinonia of Persons that exists in the Trinity. 'By communion in the Body and Blood of Christ, the faithful grow in the mystical divinisation which makes them dwell in the Son and in the Father, through the Spirit.'[342] The Eucharist manifests *par excellence* koinonia in all its aspects.[343] The source of koinonia is the Holy Spirit, who may be called 'the unity of the Trinity' as he is the love of the Father and the Son, which unites them.

In all this, we notice that for the Orthodox the Eucharist is communion with the divine Persons of the Trinity rather than *union with Christ*. Perhaps this is because the Orthodox put less emphasis on the real presence of Christ's body and blood in the Eucharist than Catholics do. This in turn may be connected with the Eastern emphasis on the *epiclesis* of the Holy Spirit rather than on the words of consecration. We need to give due weight to the creative power of God's word at the consecration, which Paul VI highlights in *Mysterium Fidei*, side by side with stress on the role of the Holy Spirit in transforming bread and wine.[344] This point also applies to the Agreed Statement of ARCIC, which said: 'bread and wine become the body and blood of Christ by the action of the Holy Spirit' (10). The Orthodox seem to relate the Eucharist directly to the Trinity and rather pass by the humanity of Christ,

---

341. *Mystery* I 5d.
342. *One in 2000?*, p. 39.
343. Ibid., p. 4.
344. See *Mystery* I 5c.

which is our way to the Father (cf. Jn 14:6) and is the source of life for us as it is united to divine nature in him (cf. Jn 6:57). It is the Word made *flesh* who St John says is 'full of *grace* and truth' (1:14).

In summary, then, the term *koinonia*, which the Orthodox also favour for describing the relation of the local churches one to another, helps us to consider the relation of the Eucharist to the Church and of the individual to the Trinity. The communion of divine Persons in the unity of the Trinity is the model for the community of persons in the unity of the Church. This unity is brought about by the Holy Spirit, by whose action the gifts of bread and wine are transformed in the Eucharist. In Orthodox theology, the Eucharist seems to be the sacrament of the life of love in the Trinity rather than primarily of the Body and Blood of Christ. In the theology of the Western Church, however, the former is communicated through receiving the latter, as we shall see in the next and final chapter.

Chapter 8

The Eucharist in our Daily Lives

So far in this book we have considered the objective reality of the Eucharist: what the Eucharist is in itself. In our final chapter, we shall consider what the Eucharist does *for us*: in other words, its purpose and the benefits of receiving it. Some of these effects have already been mentioned: union with Christ and the unity of Christ's mystical body, the Church, at the beginning of chapter five. The effects of the Eucharist will be described here under seven headings: union with Christ, the unity of the Church, charity, the forgiveness of sins, spiritual food, the indwelling of the Trinity and the resurrection of the body.

Union with Christ

It is only to be expected that the social dimension of the Eucharist as the sacrament of the unity of the Church should be given most attention in the time after the Second Vatican Council, which focussed mainly on the nature of the Church herself. I would call this the horizontal dimension of communion. But, as already noted in chapter five, the primary effect of this sacrament is union with Christ, whose body and blood we receive. I call this the vertical dimension, for it has greater depth. The most important truth about Eucharist, Fr Colman O'Neill writes, is that it unites us to the person of Christ.[345] Pope John Paul II confirms this when he says, 'The Eucharist thus appears as the culmination of all the sacraments in perfecting our communion with God the Father by identification with his only-begotten Son through the working of

---

345. *Meeting Christ in the Sacraments*, p. 184.

the Holy Spirit.'[346] His perspective is different from that of O'Neill, for it is Trinitarian, but it is by 'identification' with the Son.

There is no real union with Christ through the Eucharist unless the Eucharist is his real body and blood. We could not speak of union with Christ in the same way if the Eucharist were only a sign or figure of his body but not his true body. The result of union with Christ is that we share in his life. As Jesus said, 'As I draw life from the Father, so whoever eats me will draw life through me' (Jn 6:57). 'And because the flesh of Christ is united to the Word of God himself, it has it that it is vivified, so that it is vivifying when the body is sacramentally consumed; for Christ gives life to the world by the mysteries which he completed in the flesh.'[347] The Eucharist is a source of divine life and grace. St Thomas sees a parallel between the way Christ came into the world when 'the Word was made flesh and dwelt among us, full of grace and truth' (Jn 1:14), and the effect of the Eucharist, which is likewise to bestow grace when Christ comes into us sacramentally in communion.[348] For St Thomas, the effect of sacramental communion is threefold: we receive Christ's body and blood; these have the same effect in our spiritual life as food and drink do in our natural life; and they bring about the unity of many.[349] Thus the Eucharist causes a double union: with Christ and with one another in his body, the Church. The second follows from the first.

The Unity of the Church

The unity of the Church expressed by the Eucharist derives from the personal union of each of her members with Christ, because the more we are one with Christ the greater will be our charity and, hence, our union with anyone else. Communion both strengthens our union with Christ and with his mystical body, the Church, in

---

346. *Ecclesia de Eucharistia* 4, 34.
347. *Super Ioannem* c. 6 lect. 4 (914).
348. ST 3a 79, 1.
349. Ibid., 3a 79, 1 ad 2.

'the bond of charity' (Col 3:14). The unity of the Church is signified by the bread used for the Eucharist, since she is made up of many members just as bread is made out of many grains of wheat (1 Cor 10:17). St Thomas says that we participate in the unity of the Church through the Eucharist. We can see this effect of the sacrament, he says, from the nature of the elements used in it: as bread is made from many grains, and wine from the juice that flows from many grapes, so many are brought together into unity through the Eucharist.[350] As noted in the previous chapter, this unity is also effected by the Holy Spirit, who is called down upon the gifts of bread and wine at the *epiclesis*.

The Eucharist, however, presupposes communion with the Church, for it expresses the unity of the Church. John Paul II notes that this communion is also *visible*. The celebration of the Eucharist, which manifests the communion of the Church, also requires the outward, visible bonds of communion with the Church.[351] The Eucharist not only strengthens our union with the visible Church but also our communion with the Church in heaven. This is clear from the liturgy of the Eastern and Western Church, which both mention the Virgin Mary, the Mother of Jesus Christ our Lord and God, the apostles, martyrs and all the saints in their anaphoras or Eucharistic Prayers.[352]

Christ speaks about the unity of the Church in the parable of the true Vine, which he told at the Last Supper when the Eucharist was instituted (Jn 15:1-11). This parable well illustrates the relation of Christ's real body to his mystical body, for the Vine is Christ himself and we are the branches united with the true Vine. The parable is an exhortation to remain in Christ and to remain in charity. The two are the same thing: to remain attached to the Vine is to remain in charity. For St John, to be in charity is especially to be in the unity of the Church. It is significant

350. ST 3a 79, 1.
351. *Ecclesia de Eucharistia* 4, 35 and 38.
352. Ibid., 1, 19.

that the word 'remain', which may also be translated as abide or dwell in, occurs no less than ten times within the eleven verses of this parable. To abide in love is to remain in the Vine, and to remain in the Vine is to dwell in Christ, for Christ is the true Vine. We remain united to the Vine, and so draw life and grace from the humanity of Christ, especially through the Eucharist. As to remain in the Vine is to remain in charity, this brings us to the next effect of the Eucharist: charity.

The Sacrament of Charity

The Eucharist is called 'the sacrament of charity', as baptism is the sacrament of faith. 'The Eucharist is specially the sacrament of unity and charity.'[353] Successive popes have exhorted us to go to the Eucharist as to the fount of charity. It is the sacrament of charity because it represents the Passion of Christ, who displayed his great love for us above all in giving up his life for us on the cross. John Paul II opens his encyclical on the Eucharist by saying that in the Sacrament of the Altar the Church 'discovers the full manifestation of his (Christ's) boundless love.'[354] He goes on to say that the love shown in the Eucharist is a love that goes to the end,[355] just as St John begins his account of the Last Supper by saying that Jesus 'having loved his own in the world, he loved them to the end' (Jn 13:1). He instituted the Eucharist as a sign of the passion he was about to undergo and of the sacrifice he was to offer on the Cross. We grow in charity by commemorating Christ's supreme act of love on earth in the Eucharist.

The Eucharist does not just increase our charity but also strengthens all three of the supernatural virtues in us. The prayer after communion for the First Sunday of Lent says, 'we are refreshed by the bread from heaven, by which faith is nourished,

---

353. Aquinas, *In 1 Cor* c. 11 lect. 5 (654).
354. Op. cit., 1.
355. Ibid., 1, 11.

hope is advanced and charity is strengthened.' The charity we receive from its source in the Eucharist is not just for ourselves but meant to be useful for others as well. So it leads to action in helping others. Thus we pray that the Eucharist may have an effect in our lives by producing, which is literally bringing forth, the fruit of charity: 'Joined to you by perpetual charity, may we bear fruit that always remains.'[356] This is the 'much fruit' that we bear if we remain in Christ, the true Vine (Jn 15:5). Charity remains forever in heaven (1 Cor 13:13).

As the Eucharist, in the saying of St Augustine, is 'the bond of charity', it is also the sacrament of *peace*. The peace it especially brings comes from the forgiveness of sins.

Forgiveness of Sins

St Thomas Aquinas says that, since the Eucharist is the sacrament of the Lord's passion, whatever is the effect of the Lord's Passion is also wholly the effect of the Eucharist, 'for this sacrament is nothing else than the application of the Lord's passion to us.'[357] O'Neill says that the significance of the sacraments is that they are the means whereby Christ applies the fruits of redemption to us.[358] As the Eucharist represents the passion of Christ, so it works in the recipient what Christ's passion did for the world: his blood was poured out for the remission of sins.[359] The consecration of Christ's blood, St Thomas says, expresses the power (*virtus*) of Christ's passion. This power is twofold: the forgiveness of sins and the life of glory, which we enter by sharing in Christ's passion, just as Christ had to suffer and so enter into his glory (Lk 24:26).[360] By making present again the sacrifice that Christ offered on the cross, the Eucharist makes available all the fruits of

---

356. Postcommunion prayer, 13th Sunday of the Year.
357. *Super Ioannem* c. 6 lect 6.
358. *Meeting Christ in the Sacraments*, p. 189.
359. Aquinas, ST I3a 79, 1; cf. Mt 26:28.
360. *In 1 Cor* c. 11 lect. 6 (682).

redemption that Christ won for us. The Eucharist is also powerful for many for whom it is offered, for the dead as well as the living, besides those who consume it. This is what we mean by the sacrifice of the Eucharist also being *propitiatory*. The Eucharist works the effects of Christ's passion in us, because it is the sacrament of his body which he gave up for us, and of his blood which he 'shed for many for the forgiveness of sins'.

Here the symbolism of the bread also helps us to understand this effect of the Eucharist. The use of bread in the Eucharist reminds us that Christ once compared himself with the grain of wheat that falls into the ground and dies. 'Unless a grain of wheat falls into the ground and dies, it remains a single grain; but if it dies it bears much fruit' (Jn 12:24). This fruit is the fruit of the Passion and Redemption. In receiving Christ in the Eucharist, we also receive all the fruits of his passion, death and resurrection, for he is the grain of wheat that fell into the ground and died, and by rising from the tomb of the ground bore much fruit.

The fruits of his passion are: to be freed from sin and reconciled with God in the peace made by the cross 'so making peace, that he might reconcile us both to God in one body through the cross' (Eph 2:16). Christ frees us by paying the price of our redemption, which is his precious blood. ('Precious' comes from the Latin word *pretium*, which means a price.) Redemption literally means to buy back; it was the technical term used for buying back prisoners of war from slavery. As the Israelites were redeemed from slavery in Egypt by sacrificing a Paschal lamb, so we have been redeemed from sin by the sacrifice of Christ at the feast of the Passover. Thus he is our Paschal lamb, who takes away the sin of the world (Jn 1:29). 'You were ransomed with the *precious* blood of Christ, like that of a lamb without spot' (1 Pet 1: 18). Christ did more than enough to redeem us by shedding his blood on the cross. In his poem *Caritas nimia* (exceeding love), Richard Crashaw coins the word 'overbought':

'What is man that you overbought / Such a thing of nought?'

For one drop of his blood would have been enough to save the whole world and take away the sins of all time.

> *Cuius una stilla salvum facere*
> *Totum mundum quit ab omni scelere*

Literally: of which (his blood) one drop is able to save the whole world from every crime, St Thomas says in the *Adoro te devote*.

Christ's passion works in those who receive it with charity. What St Paul says is especially true of the Eucharist: 'he was set forth as an expiation for sins to be received with faith' (Rom 3:25). For the Eucharist to be effective this faith needs to be 'formed by charity' (Gal 5:6). The Eucharist only brings forgiveness of daily, lesser sins, which do not destroy charity, for 'charity covers a multitude of sins' (1 Pet 4:8). But the Eucharist does not forgive mortal sin, which altogether quenches the charity of the Holy Spirit, for one needs to be in a state of grace and charity to receive it in the first place. The Eucharist cannot by itself restore us to charity when it has been altogether lost. For this we need the sacrament of penance. The Eucharist cannot put us into a state of grace when it has been lost, because it is the visible sign of being in grace and charity.

St Thomas distinguishes the ways the fruits of the sacrifice benefit those who receive communion and those for whom Mass is offered. He starts by saying that the Eucharist is a sacrifice and it is a sacrament. It is a sacrifice as it is offered, a sacrament as it is consumed (eaten). The sacrament directly has the effect for which it was instituted. This, he says, was not for satisfying sin but for spiritual nourishment by union with Christ and the members of his body. This unity is made by charity. The one who receives the Eucharist obtains remission of sin through the fervour of his or her charity. The Eucharist satisfies for those for whom it is offered according to the amount of their devotion, not the amount of what is offered; it does not take away all punishment of sin.[361]

---

361. ST 3a 79,5.

Spiritual Food

As we need to eat and drink in order to sustain our bodily life, so we have a sacrament of eating and drinking for our spiritual life. Thus the Eucharist provides us with food to nourish the life of our souls. St Ambrose derives the reason for this from the Real Presence: 'It is Christ who is in this sacrament, because it is the body of Christ. Therefore, it is not corporeal but spiritual food.'[362] He then quotes St Paul: 'Our fathers ate spiritual food and drank spiritual drink' (1 Cor 10:3). We can tell this effect, St Thomas says, from the way in which the sacrament is given: as food and drink. The Eucharist has all the effects in our spiritual life that ordinary food does for our natural life: it sustains our strength, increases growth, replenishes lost strength and provides delight. The Eucharist brings spiritual delight, just as the bread from heaven, which the Israelites ate in the desert, contained every delight and was suited to every taste (Wis 16:20).

The bread from heaven (manna) is also the bread of angels: 'He gave them bread from heaven; men ate the bread of angels' (Ps 77:24). The bread of angels has been made the bread of travellers, or wayfarers, on the journey through life on earth:

> *Ecce panis angelorum*
> *Factus cibus viatorum.*

'Behold the bread of angels has been made the food of wayfarers.'[363] Since Christ is hidden from our sight in the Eucharist, only apprehended by faith, he is 'the hidden manna' (Rev 2:17). The angels in heaven feed their minds on the sight of him who is hidden from our sight in the sacrament of the Eucharist. As St Thomas explains: 'Christ is contained in this sacrament not in his own appearance but in the appearance of the sacrament.' 'The angels eat (feed on) Christ in his own appearance, inasmuch as they are united to him by the enjoyment of perfect charity and clear vision,

---

362. *De Mysteriis* 58.
363. *Lauda, Sion*, the Sequence for Corpus Christi.

which bread we expect in our heavenly homeland (*in patria*), not in faith, as we are now united to him.'[364] Aquinas says that the Eucharist is called 'the bread of angels' because what is ordered to an end derives from it. Our reception of the Eucharist, he says, is ordered to the end of enjoying the sight of Christ in his own appearance in our heavenly homeland, which is the enjoyment that the angels in heaven have of him. The angels enjoy this bread (Christ is the bread who came down from heaven) in its own appearance; so St Thomas says that it is primarily the bread of angels and secondarily of men and women.[365] Human beings, he says, belong to the society of the mystical body of Christ by faith, and angels by open vision. The sacraments are adapted to faith, by which St Thomas says the truth is seen as in a mirror and in an enigma or riddle, quoting 1 Cor 13:12.

The bread of angels has become the food of travellers. The Eucharist is food to sustain us on the journey of our life through this world, just as Elijah found scones on a stone in the desert and was told, 'Arise and eat, or the journey will be too great for you' (1 Kgs 19:7). And with the strength of this food he walked for forty days and nights until he reached Mount Horeb. Christ walks at our side, John Paul II remarks, hidden beneath the lowly signs of bread and wine, just as he accompanied the two disciples on the road to Emmaus towards evening.[366] St John of the Cross calls the Eucharist by allusion 'the supper that refreshes'. Commenting on the text: 'I stand outside and knock, and if anyone hears me and opens the door, I shall come in to share my meal with him' (Rev 3:20), he writes:

> He (God) is himself for her (the soul) the supper which recreates and enkindles love.[367]

Although the author refers to the effects of prayer, these words

---

364. ST 3a 80, 2.
365. Ibid., 3a 80, 2 as 1.
366. *Ecclesia de Eucharistia* 62; cf. Lk 24:15.
367. *Spiritual Canticle* 14/15, 29 (A Peers trans., vol. 2, p. 274).

may well be applied to the Eucharist.

The Eucharist is spiritual food; it has the opposite effect of ordinary food. As St Augustine noted, it is not changed into us but we are changed into, or made more like, what we receive. In the post-communion prayer for the 27th Sunday, we ask God that he feeds us 'until we cross over into that which we consume.' We may add with St Paul: 'until Christ is formed in us' (Gal 4:19).

The Indwelling of the Trinity

Since one of the effects of the Eucharist is that Christ dwells in us and we in him,[368] and Christ is in his Father and the Father in him,[369] it follows that whoever receives the Eucharist with charity has all three Persons of the Trinity dwelling in him or her, because Christ dwells in him or her. For whoever has the Father and the Son also has the Holy Spirit, who is inseparable from them because he is their mutual love. By sharing in the Eucharist, we are made partakers of the divine nature: 'Lord, as you feed us with the food of your sacred body and blood, make us partakers of the divine nature.'[370] By receiving his body and blood we draw divine life from Christ through his humanity, just as he drew life from his Father through the union of his human nature to divine nature in him: 'As I draw life from the Father, so whoever eats me will draw life through me' (Jn 6:57). To share in divine life is to share in the life of the whole Trinity, for the Father, Son and Holy Spirit are inseparable, though distinct, Persons. We cannot have any one of them without the other two, since each is in the other. The Father is in the Son and Son in the Father, and the Holy Spirit proceeds from them both, because he is the love of them both. As Christ is in the Father and we in Christ, so we are in the Father and the Father in us, with their Holy Spirit.[371] Thus the dwelling

---

368. Jn 6:56.
369. Ibid., 14:10, 17:21.
370. Post-communion, 28th Sunday.
371. Jn 14:20.

of the Son in the Father is the pattern for our dwelling in Christ, according to St John. The indwelling of the three Persons of the Trinity in one another (known as their 'circumincession'), is also the pattern of Christ dwelling in us.

This connection between the Eucharist and the Trinity is clearly portrayed for us in Rublëv's famous icon of the Trinity, depicted as three angels, for the angels share in the meal of bread provided for them by Abraham (Gen 18:2f). By sharing in the living bread of the Eucharist, we receive or share in the life of the Trinity.

Christ spoke about the indwelling of the Trinity in us at the Last Supper when he said: 'If anyone loves me, he will keep my commandments and my Father will love him and we shall come to him and make our dwelling with him' (Jn 14:23). Thus the indwelling of the Trinity exists wherever there is charity, which is given us through the Holy Spirit. We live out this communion with the Trinity, which we have through the Eucharist, in our daily lives by being in union with others.[372]

In accord with the tradition of the Eastern Church, which we noted at the end of the previous chapter, Pope John Paul II has emphasised the relation of the Eucharist to the Holy Spirit. 'Through communion in his body and blood, Christ also grants us his Spirit.'[373] He observes that 'the inseparable activity of the Son and of the Holy Spirit ... is at work in the Eucharist.'[374] We first call down the Spirit, the source of every gift, at the *epiclesis*.

We both receive the Spirit of Christ by being joined to his body, and the Spirit makes us one body with him. We have Christ's Spirit by being part of his body, just as body and soul are united in a human person. St Augustine tells his flock: 'let them be the body of Christ if they wish to live by the Spirit of Christ.'[375] The giving of the Holy Spirit flows from Christ's sacrifice. In Jan van

---

372. CCC 2485.
373. *Ecclesia de Eucharistia* 1, 17.
374. Ibid., 2, 23.
375. *In Ioannem* Tract 26, 13.

Eyck's great painting of the Adoration of the Lamb, the fountain of water that symbolises the Holy Spirit is placed in the foreground beneath the altar at the centre of the picture, on which stands the Lamb as though slain, with blood flowing from his wounded breast into a chalice on the altar, standing for the Eucharist. Van Eyck's painting recalls the scene at the end of the Apocalypse: 'Then he showed me the river of the water of life flowing from the throne of God and of the lamb' (Rev 22:1). St John of the Cross says that we find this eternal fountain hidden in the living bread of the Eucharist, which is Christ himself:

Aquesta eterna fonte está escondida
En este vivo pan por darnos vida.

That eternal fount is hidden in this living bread, to give us life.[376]

The Resurrection

Christ explicitly links the Eucharist with our future resurrection: 'And I shall raise him up on the last day' (Jn 6:40). He repeats this four times in the Discourse on the Bread of Life: also John 6:39, 44 and 54. We saw in chapter two that from early times the Fathers, especially Irenaeus, associated the Eucharist with the resurrection of the body. St Ignatius of Antioch called the Eucharist 'the medicine of immortality'.[377] The Eucharist brings about our resurrection because, as Christ's body was raised to life again, so whoever partakes of his risen body will be raised up again. We recall that the Eucharist contains Christ's body as it now is, risen and glorified. John Paul II drew attention to the truth that the Eucharist is not just the memorial of Christ's death but also of his resurrection. As a consequence, 'When the Church celebrates the Eucharist, the memorial of the Lord's death and resurrection, this central event of salvation becomes really present.'[378] 'Christ's passover includes not

---

376. *Poems* VIII (Que bien sé yo la fonte: How well I know the fountain).
377. *Ad Ephesos* 20.
378. *Ecclesia de Eucharistia* 1, 11.

only his passion and death, but also his resurrection ... The Eucharistic sacrifice makes present not only the mystery of the Saviour's passion and death, but also the mystery of the resurrection which crowned the sacrifice.'[379] In the same paragraph, Pope John Paul remarks that Christ is "the bread of life" as the living and risen One.

The Eucharist preserves us for the resurrection of the body, because it heals the *whole* person in this life, body and soul. The resurrection of the body will be the final *re-integration* of our human nature, when the healing of it which has begun in this life by grace will be completed. Thus the Eucharist leads us to glory in the future life. It is, however, not only a pledge of future glory but also gives us a share in eternal life even now, as John Paul II himself has emphasised:

> Those who feed on Christ in the Eucharist need not wait until the hereafter to receive eternal life: *they already possess it on earth*, as the first-fruits of a future fullness which will embrace man in his totality.[380]

We should note that in St John 'eternal life' does not just mean a life in the future but means a particular *kind* of life, which we can share even now, the life of Christ that will last for ever. 'Eternal' means rather 'everlasting'. As St John writes, 'He who eats my flesh and drinks my blood has eternal life, and I will raise him up on the last day' (6:54). John Paul II comments: 'This pledge of the future resurrection comes from the fact that the flesh of the Son of Man, given as food, is his body in its glorious state after the resurrection.'[381]

For St Thomas Aquinas, *every* communion is *viaticum,* that is, food for travellers on their way through this world towards glory in the next life. The Eucharist leads us to glory, because it is, as John Paul II says, the memorial of Christ's death and resurrection. St Thomas sees the Eucharist working in us what Christ did by his death and resurrection:

---

379. Ibid., 1, 14.
380. Ibid., 1, 18 (his italics).
381. Ibid., 1, 18.

Whence it is manifest that the destruction of death, which Christ destroyed by dying, and the restoring of life, which he worked by rising again, are the effects of this sacrament.[382]

In the view of St Thomas, the Eucharist also leads us to our resurrection, because it makes us participate in the Holy Spirit: 'The Eucharist leads to the resurrection, because whoever eats and drinks of it spiritually is made a participator in the Holy Spirit, and God will raise up those who have the Holy Spirit dwelling in them, according to Romans 8:11: "and if the Spirit of him who raised Jesus from the dead dwells in you, then he who raised Jesus from the dead will give life to your mortal bodies through the Holy Spirit dwelling in you".'[383] Since the glorified Christ is present in the Eucharist, so the life we share in the Eucharist is his risen life. Thus every communion is an eating and drinking with the risen Lord, just as the disciples ate and drank with the risen Christ during the 40 days after his Resurrection. As St Peter proclaimed to the household of Cornelius in Caesarea: 'God raised him up on the third day and made him manifest, not to all the people but to us who were chosen by God to be his witnesses, who ate and drank with him after he rose from the dead' (Acts 10:41).

All three aspects of the Eucharist, past, present and future, are summed up for us in the Magnificat antiphon for the feast of Corpus Christi:

O sacred banquet in which Christ is eaten, the memory of his passion is renewed, the soul is filled with grace and a pledge of future glory is given.

This antiphon reminds us of the main parts of the doctrine of the Eucharist. It is a sacrifice as it makes present again Christ's passion in the past. It contains Christ really present, who is full of grace. It gives us the promise of glory in the life to come. Commenting

---

382. *Super Ioannem* c. 6 lect. 6 (965).
383. Ibid., c. 6 lect. 7 (973).

on Hebrews 10:20, St Thomas remarks that, as the priests of the Old Covenant entered the Holy of Holies once a year through the veil of the Temple, so we enter the heavenly sanctuary by a new and living way through the veil of Christ's flesh. He adds: 'His flesh is given under the veil of the appearances of bread in this sacrament.'[384] Christ's humanity is also the door by which we enter into the sheepfold of eternal life; [385] by feeding us with his own body and blood, Christ the shepherd leads us into eternal life, which we share even now.

However wonderful the mystery of the Eucharist is, a time will come when the sacrament is no longer necessary, for Christ will no more be hidden from our sight beneath the appearances of bread and wine but we shall see him face to face in open vision. Then indeed 'our soul shall be filled with the sight of his glory' (Ps 62:5). St Thomas used to pray before Mass that he 'come to see *revealed* face to face what he was about to receive *veiled* on the way.'

Our way to glory in the future life is none other than the one that was taken by Christ, who had to die in order to enter into glory (Lk 24:26). This was by the Paschal mystery of his passion, death and resurrection, which we commemorate every time we celebrate the Eucharist. What Christ did by dying and rising in his body, has to be done in us through the sacraments. By sharing in his body and blood, which were sacrificed on the cross for us, we are brought to the glory of his resurrection. The Paschal mystery will be completed in us when our bodies are raised up to glory, which is the goal of the Eucharist.

> O Jesus, whom I now look on concealed,
> I pray that what I long for be done,
> That seeing you revealed face to face,
> I may be blessed with the vision of your glory.[386]

---

384. *Super Hebraeos* c. 10 lect. 2.
385. Jn 10:9.
386. Aquinas, *Adoro te devote.*

Bibliography

ARCIC, Anglican Roman Catholic International Commission, *The Final Report*. London, CTS/SPCK 1982.

Clark, F., *Eucharistic Sacrifice and the Reformation*. London, Darton Longman & Todd 1960.

Jeremias, J., *The Eucharistic Words of Jesus*. London, SCM 1966.

John Paul II, *Ecclesia de Eucharistia* (2003).

Journet, C., *La Messe. Présence du Sacrifice de la Croix*. Paris, Desclée de Brouwer 1958.

Kodell, J., *The Eucharist in the New Testament*. Collegeville, Liturgical Press 1998.

Lubac, H. de, *Corpus Mysticum*. Paris, Aubier 1949.
The Splendour of the Church. London, Sheed & Ward 1956.

McPartlan, P., *The Eucharist. The Body of Christ*. London, CTS 2004.
The Eucharist Makes the Church. Edinburgh, T & T Clark 1993.
One in 2000? London, St Pauls 1993.
Sacrament of Salvation. Edinburgh, T & T Clark 1995.

Moloney, R., *The Eucharist*. London, Chapman 1995.

Nichols, A., *The Holy Eucharist*. Dublin, Veritas 1991.

O'Connor, J., *The Hidden Manna*. San Francisco, Ignatius Press 1998.

O'Neill, C., *Meeting Christ in the Sacraments*. Cork, Mercier 1964.
New Approaches to the Eucharist. Dublin, Gill 1967.

Paul VI, *Mysterium Fidei* (1965).

Pius XII, *Mediator Dei* (1947).

Schillebeeckx, E., *The Eucharist*. London, Sheed & Ward 1968.

Vatican II, *Lumen Gentium* (1964).
Sacrosanctum Concilium (1963).

World Council of Churches, *Baptism, Eucharist and Ministry*. Geneva, 1982.

Index